D1520617

SAGE Guide to Careers for Counseling and Clinical Practice

To every person whose identity has been forged—day-after-day, job-after-job, client-after-client—by their choice and dedication to "always becoming" a counselor.

SAGE Guide to Careers for Counseling and Clinical Practice

Camille Helkowski

Loyola University Chicago

Los Angeles | London | New Delhi
Singapore | Washington DC | Melbourne

FOR INFORMATION:

SAGE Publications, Inc.
2455 Teller Road
Thousand Oaks, California 91320
E-mail: order@sagepub.com

SAGE Publications Ltd.
1 Oliver's Yard
55 City Road
London EC1Y 1SP
United Kingdom

SAGE Publications India Pvt. Ltd.
B 1/I 1 Mohan Cooperative Industrial Area
Mathura Road, New Delhi 110 044
India

SAGE Publications Asia-Pacific Pte. Ltd.
3 Church Street
#10–04 Samsung Hub
Singapore 049483

Printed in the United States of America

ISBN: 978-1-5443-2707-5

This book is printed on acid-free paper.

Acquisitions Editor: Abbie Rickard
Editorial Assistant: Jennifer Cline
Production Editor: Jane Martinez
Copy Editor: Terri Lee Paulsen
Typesetter: C&M Digitals (P) Ltd.
Proofreader: Dennis W. Webb
Cover Designer: Candice Harman
Marketing Manager: Jenna Retana

SUSTAINABLE FORESTRY INITIATIVE   Certified Sourcing   www.sfiprogram.org   SFI-01075

18 19 20 21 22 10 9 8 7 6 5 4 3 2 1

CONTENTS

PREFACE

Because career satisfaction requires curiosity, when an individual says, "I want to be a counselor," we assume that their curiosity has driven them to explore the benefits and challenges of this profession and that they have come to an understanding of what it *actually means* to be a counselor. We imagine that they have asked themselves key questions about the field, investigated the range of occupations and opportunities available to them with a graduate degree in counseling, and compared their skillset and values to those demanded by the profession they wish to make their own. Unfortunately and much too often, our assumptions are wrong. The fledgling professionals we teach and supervise often remain blissfully unaware of the realities of choosing a career in counseling. It is my hope that *SAGE Guide to Careers for Counseling and Clinical Practice* helps fill the knowledge gap between wishful thinking and evidence-based decision making.

This book strives to provide basic information about the profession of counseling while it also showcases a variety of counseling-related careers that serve diverse populations in a range of settings. Perhaps the most interesting and beneficial feature of the specific career chapters is the "Meet the expert" section. These professionals have generously told their career stories and offered their perceptions and practical suggestions; while not part and parcel of Bureau of Labor Statistics information, their contributions are perhaps even more relevant.

The truth is that counseling students and new professionals need both facts and feature stories to understand what the profession has to offer and chart their course accordingly. *SAGE Guide to Careers for Counseling and Clinical Practice* endeavors to bring all the necessary elements to light.

ACKNOWLEDGMENTS

Projects like *SAGE Guide to Careers for Counseling and Clinical Practice* become deliverable because so many people graciously gave their time and talent to the process. My thanks go to Abbie Rickard at SAGE Publishing, who chose me to author this book and who was always available for questions and suggestions.

Without the enormous contributions of the counseling professionals who shared the details of their careers, there would be no book at all. While some of these experts are long-time friends, others I have never even met in person. All of them answered my call and gave me and my readers the gift of their experience and insight. I am most grateful to Jennifer Buckler, Catherine Carrigan, Louise Dimiceli-Mitran, Andrew Hrvol, Kenneth Jackson, Azizi Marshall, Diane McDonald, Cindy Montgomery, Rick Rittmaster, Antonio Romano, Matt Sheahan, Alison Toback, Serena Wadhwa, Rachel Wagner-Cantine, and Susan Wortman.

And finally, my heartfelt thanks to my friends and family, and particularly my husband, Bob, who are the unsung heroes of all my writing efforts. As always, I couldn't have done it without you!

The author and SAGE gratefully acknowledge the contributions of the following reviewers:

Deirdre Donat, *Adelphi University*

Kerrie R. Fineran, *Purdue University Fort Wayne*

Wendy Killam, *Stephen F. Austin State University*

Delishia M. Pittmann, *George Washington University*

Matthew R. Shupp, *Shippensburg University of Pennsylvania*

Beth A. Trammell, *Indiana University East*

ABOUT THE AUTHOR

Camille Helkowski, MEd, NCC, LCPC, has over 30 years of experience as a counselor, clinical supervisor, educator, writer, and presenter, with extensive work in higher education and clinical practice. Recently retired from Loyola University Chicago's Career Development Center, she is now focused on her private counseling practice in Lincolnwood, Illinois, where she provides counseling services to individuals and couples around a broad spectrum of issues including relational concerns, grief and loss, healing from trauma, career concerns across the life span, and special counseling needs of young adults.

Helkowski is a highly regarded speaker, trainer, and group facilitator and an acknowledged expert on the topics of young adult development and related transitions. Additionally, she is the coauthor of several articles and books, including: *Connect College to Career: A Student's Guide to Work and Life Transitions* with Paul Hettich and *The College Student Counseling Treatment Planner* with Chris Stout and Art Jongma. She has also designed and taught Career Counseling for Pastoral Counselors for Loyola University Chicago's Institute of Pastoral Studies MPC program and graduate courses in career theory and counseling, group counseling, and practicum seminars for Argosy University Chicago. She received her bachelor's degree from DePaul University and her master's degree in counseling from Loyola University Chicago.

WHY CHOOSE A CAREER IN COUNSELING?

What you are in love with, what seizes your imagination, will affect everything.

—Pedro Arrupe, S. J.

CAREERS BEGIN AT THE BEGINNING

I wanted to be a cowgirl. Not just any cowgirl. I wanted to be Annie Oakley. This goal may have been more likely had I grown up on a farm or ranch instead of the west side of Chicago, where the only horses to be found were in books or movies. But I was not deterred. Annie was amazing. How did I know that? Because she had her very own television show.

I grew up during the "Golden Age of Westerns." Each of the three major channels had their own star-studded lineup—all of them featuring men. Annie was the only woman with a show of her own. Actually, Annie was the only woman in a Western with a life of her own. She had her own horse, her own gun, and her own adventures. Yup . . . I wanted to be just like Annie and throughout my life I have tried to emulate what I came to understand was best about her. I gave up the idea of literally riding horses, saving settlers, and chasing outlaws as a way of life. But figuratively, my days as a counselor are filled with helping folks establish and live their lives fully. Everyone needs to feel safe and happy in their own skin. Everyone has an outlaw or two who have made their lives difficult. Everyone struggles—with the harshness of nature, with sadness and loss, with transition, with betrayal—with something. Everyone also has a shadow side. Annie did. Her need to be independent made it difficult for her to allow companionship. She believed that she couldn't have both, and perhaps, in the world she inhabited, she couldn't.

Many years later, the image of Annie Oakley still inspires me to do my best to be true to myself and be generous to and authentic with others in a world that can sometimes be difficult and feel unforgiving. And so I finally get to the questions of what and/or who inspired you as a child: Who were your heroes? Why were they important to you? When you dreamed of what you'd become as a grown-up, what were the shapes of those dreams? How did your early dreams lead you to counseling? How do they fit—right now—into work as a counselor?

Certainly, family can have a major (and sometimes complete) influence on future aspirations. What were the messages sent by your parents, grandparents, siblings? Carl Jung suggested that "The strongest psychological influence on children is the unlived life of their parents." Are your counseling aspirations an outgrowth of family demands that were constants as you were growing up? Of health, gender, or financial issues that were never resolved satisfactorily? Of parental needs that were never met? In discerning what is authentically you, Sharon Daloz Parks suggests that it is useful to hear the "still, small voice" but also to recognize that we carry with us an entire committee of voices and being a strong committee chairperson is the challenge (Parks, 2000, p. 85).

All of these questions are important to ask and answer. Not because a specific answer is a better or worse reason to choose a counseling career, but because you need to be completely clear as to why you're making the choice. In "A Path Well Chosen," an article in a recent issue of *Counseling Today*, counselors from across the United States were asked what led them to the field. Penny Mechley-Porter, a counselor in private practice in Erie, PA, responded, "I know counseling is a good fit for me because it matches who I have always been" (Bray, 2017, p. 35).

LIFE AS A COUNSELOR— COMMON THREADS

The American Counseling Association's *20/20: A Vision for the Future of Counseling* "provided profession-wide clarity as to what it means to engage in professional counseling" when it offered the following consensus definition: "Counseling is a professional relationship that empowers diverse individuals, families, and groups to accomplish mental health, wellness, education, and career goals" (Kaplan,

Tarvydas, & Gladding, 2014, p. 366). Because every key organization and professional association that represents counselors chose to embrace this definition, it
can and does speak directly to our professional identity. It signifies that counseling
is a separate and distinct profession from all other helping professions, with its own
educational and training requirements, ethical principles, and core competencies.

This definition also translates into a myriad of specific careers based on a range
of variables including an individual's personal values, skillset, and career goals;
education attained; and lifestyle preferred. Under the large occupational umbrella
called "counseling" there are a host of options. While this book will outline several, there are many more to consider. Also, it's helpful to keep in mind that many
counselors have been able to customize roles to truly fit their specific professional
interests and career aspirations.

Calling and Meaning Making

"If you understand the ways in which the person you are and the needs of the
larger world intersect, you have some idea about your calling. The question then
broadens from 'what can I do that will make me happy?' to 'what can I do that
will give me purpose?'" (Hettich & Helkowski, 2005, p. 146). If you filled a ball-
room with people from all realms of the counseling world and asked them "How
did you come to choose this career?," almost all of their responses would include
the concept of "helping people" as the prime determinant of their vocation. They
may differentiate the types of people they'd most like to help or the ways in which
they believe that help can best be provided, but helping others is at the heart of
their career decision. Most would also suggest that this is the work they were
called to—work where they found meaning and discovered their purpose.

As the millennium approached, a change occurred in the way traditional
counseling was conceptualized and practiced. Counselors recognized that the
barriers clients faced in obtaining care and needed services must be removed and
that issues of social justice and advocacy needed to be addressed by the profession
itself. Counselors began to see themselves not only as helping others but also as
instruments of societal change. Counselors for Social Justice became an officially
recognized division of the American Counseling Association (ACA) in 2002 and
made social justice a clear priority for the field. In 2003 the ACA identified specific competencies counselors must possess to advocate successfully. In September
2017 a search on the ACA website for "advocacy" and "social justice" brings up
10 books, 461 articles in *Counseling Today*, 236 articles in the *Journal of Counseling and Development*, 22 podcasts, and 9 webinars. The profession of counseling

embraces advocacy in education, thought, research, and action and proves itself to be a home for those whose purpose is as much societal as individual.

It's Personal: Experience and Shipwrecks

In my more than 30 years of work as a counselor specializing in career issues, I have heard many reasons why people have chosen to pursue a career in counseling. Many feel as though they have been doing this work most of their lives. They are the folks that friends and family seem to gravitate to when times are tough. It is difficult, especially for individuals with limited experience, to understand that while their intentions were good, it is very likely that they were sharing their opinions and essentially telling those who came to them what to do. And, while sometimes advice-giving is helpful to people, it is not counseling. In fact, using this kind of experience as the sole rationale for choosing to be a counselor makes as much sense as becoming an attorney because you've always liked to argue. In both cases, these experiences represent something associated with the profession but certainly not enough to make a commitment to it or to believe it is your destiny.

Does your personal experience count in making this career choice? Of course it does. But the experiences you should be looking to are those that cultivate a worldview, micro-skills, and competencies that are in line with the counseling profession. Involve yourself in work that fosters relational skills. Put yourself in roles and organizations that promote cultural competence. Learn more about the field by joining professional associations, reading, and developing relationships with counselors who are doing the type of work that interests you. Ask questions of others and of yourself. Reflect on your personal and professional development and compare your findings to the professional identity of the field. Whether there is a good fit or an uncomfortable one, it is information that is necessary for solid career decision-making.

On the flip side, we often seek to emulate someone who has been there for us through difficult times or circumstances. In particular, we are drawn to the professions those individuals inhabited. If you have used the services of a counselor and those services have been effective in helping you through a shipwreck or transition, it is not unusual to consider becoming a counselor. A shipwreck—and we all have them—is Parks's description of a loss that changes everything and leaves us depleted. It irrevocably reorders life by calling into question "things as we have perceived them. Or as they were taught to us, or as we had read, heard, or assumed. This kind of experience can suddenly rip into the fabric of life, or it may slowly yet just as surely unravel the meanings that have served as the home of the soul" (Parks, 2000, p. 28).

Rebuilding a life is a process, and many of us seek help moving through it. If that help came from a counselor, then why not pay it forward? That is an excellent question, and for some the response is "why not, indeed!" But for others, the distinction between being helped and doing the helping is significant.

For example, I have a considerable sweet tooth and there's nothing I love more than an exceptional chocolate donut. There is a wonderful family-run bakery very close to my office, and some days my car just turns into the parking lot to satisfy my donut cravings. And while I love everything about this bakery, I actually hate baking. I don't like the time and energy it takes to follow a recipe specifically, measure accurately, or preheat the oven. So I leave it to the professionals, and I simply enjoy the fruits of their labor of love. The point is that it is not enough to choose a counseling career because you loved your results when you worked with a counselor. You also have to want to spend your days doing what a counselor does!

The Impact of World Events

National and global events both suggest and shape careers. In the early 1960s, John F. Kennedy inspired American youth to "ask what you can do for your country." He established the Peace Corps on March 1, 1961, and within six years the Corps had attracted 14,500 volunteers to programs in 55 developing countries. Since that time, over 220,000 Americans have joined the Peace Corps and responded to President Kennedy's original challenge (https://www.peacecorps .gov/about/history/founding-moment).

September 11, 2001, was, for some, another kind of national call. Post-9/11, applications to the CIA and FBI rose significantly as did interest in all federal, state, and local law enforcement agencies. In the face of this national tragedy, the need for counselors also increased as people sought out ways to make meaning of the events of that day.

In the last year alone, we have faced a contentious presidential election—communities divided by issues of race, immigration, economic parity, and environmental disasters. Right now ACA's home page is asking counselors from across the country to mobilize in response to the victims of hurricanes that have ravaged parts of Texas, Florida, and all of Puerto Rico. Individuals seeking a profession that will allow them to make a difference on a national as well as local level are right to consider counseling.

LOOKING FORWARD

Much like human development, careers have stages as well. In their December 2013 article for the American College Personnel Association website, Londoño-McConnell and Matthews outline a model of career development for counselors. While the article is specific to university counseling centers, I think it generalizes well. The authors call the first stage The Young Guns. These are the highly motivated new professionals who are anxious to practice what they have learned in graduate school. They are testing the waters of the profession and may try their hand at a range of professional options. They are working to become competent, get licensed, and reduce their reliance on external expertise to do their jobs. They also look for professional recognition and work/life balance.

Crossroads Counselors (Stage 2) have been in the field for 6–10 years and are facing important professional decisions. Should they stay in this area of the field or is it time to move on? Should they expand their range of professional involvement or contract the number of activities in which they're immersed? Motivated to achieve and grow in a career with short career ladders, they run the risk of taking on too much and experiencing burnout or compassion fatigue. This stage is a time for deep reflection and clarifying their professional identity.

A counselor in the field for 10–16 years has entered Stage 3: The Next Generation. This stage, hallmarked by changing job descriptions and relationships with colleagues and clients alike, can offer potential for supervising and mentoring of younger counselors. Erik Erickson's Theory of Psychosocial Development calls it generativity. Counselors with this level of experience need to clarify their professional and personal priorities to keep their passion for the field burning brightly.

The Seasoned Sage (Stage 4) finds new challenge and growth in the work by staying on top of the latest professional developments and diversifying their experience. Counselors at this stage know that they can trust their internal expertise. "Over time, experience-based generalizations and accumulated wisdom replace the use of 'external' sources of expertise and prescribed way of doing things. In this sense, the 'seasoned' professional has their own body of knowledge that they rely on much more heavily in the work" (Londoño-McConnell & Matthews, 2013).

The lifelong impact of a counseling career upon the counselor is difficult to specify or quantify. However, if you still believe that a counseling career is worth considering or continuing, perhaps Samuel Gladding provides us with the best answer to the question, "Why counseling?"

> It (counseling) looks at reality and accepts what is, but it doesn't stay there. Counseling offers three ways of dealing with what stands before us. It offers *care* in the form of knowing how to respond and when to act. It offers *creativity* in helping people put their lives back together in a way that is ever new, ever changing, and productive. Finally, it offers *hope* both in what we can be and who we can help others become. The holistic view of humankind that counseling offers goes beyond the mundane and the tragic that all too often fill the world. The possible and productive side of counseling call out to a world in chaos that there is hope that comes in the form of listening, understanding, and responding in ways that bridge gaps instead of create them. (Gladding, 2009, p. 303; emphasis in original)

References

Bray, B. (2017, December). A path well chosen. *Counseling Today, 60*(3), 26–37.

Gladding, S. T. (2009). *Becoming a counselor: The light, the bright, and the serious.* Alexandria, VA: American Counseling Association Foundation.

Hettich, P. I., & Helkowski, C. (2005). *Connect college to career: A student's guide to work and life transitions.* Belmont, CA: Thomson/Wadsworth.

Kaplan, D. M., Tarvydas, V. M., & Gladding, S. T. (2014, July). 20/20: A vision for the future of counseling: The new consensus definition of counseling. *Journal of Counseling & Development, 92,* 366–372.

Londoño-McConnell, A., & Matthews, J. K. (2013, December 31). Seasons of a counselor's life: Career development of professional staff in counseling centers. Retrieved from http://www.myacpa.org/sites/default/files/ccapsSeasons%20of%20a%20Counselors%20Life.pdf

Parks, S. D. (2000). *Big questions, worthy dreams.* San Francisco, CA: Jossey-Bass.

AVENUES TO COUNSELING CAREERS

EDUCATIONAL REQUIREMENTS AND CHOICES: THE BIG PICTURE

According to the American Counseling Association (ACA) website, "Professional Counselors are graduate level (either master's or doctoral degree) mental health service providers, trained to work with individuals, families, and groups in treating mental, behavioral, and emotional problems and disorders." It goes on to say that a professional counselor will possess a master's or doctoral degree from a range of counseling disciplines (https://www.counseling.org/careers/aca-career-central/choosing-a-career-in-counseling).

The good news is that the educational prerequisites to become a counselor are fairly straightforward. First, you obtain a bachelor's degree. Generally, people who become counselors have done an undergraduate degree majoring in a liberal arts discipline; however, you can enter a counseling program with any undergraduate major. I have met accountants and engineers who have chosen to become counselors.

Next, you obtain a master's degree from a counseling program. The programs are varied and are offered by traditional four-year universities and schools of professional psychology. There are also online or distance learning master's programs available. The program you choose will depend on a range of factors: Your specific professional interests, cost and availability of graduate assistantships and financial aid, geographic location, accreditation, and practice and research interests of the faculty are all considerations.

Once you have a master's degree, should you go on for a PhD? It depends. Most practitioners are educated at the master's level because a master's degree in counseling is a practical degree that prepares graduates to become licensed counselors. A master's-prepared counselor can specialize in a variety of counseling careers, including school counseling, marriage and family counseling, rehabilitation counseling, substance abuse counseling, or mental health counseling. Master's degree programs require a blend of coursework in psychology, culture, and practice and hands-on experience in the counseling field. Typically, a master's degree can be completed in two years of full-time work (Buffardi, 2010).

Individuals who pursue a doctorate in counseling psychology are generally motivated by specific career goals in research, consulting, or independent practice. They may also wish to pursue faculty positions in psychology, counseling, or human services programs and/or have an interest in counselor education and supervision or university administration. It typically takes five years to complete a PhD in counseling psychology.

LEARNING BY DOING

A key element of any counseling curriculum is practical experience. It is also critical in deciding which counseling program is best for you. The types of experience required, especially at the master's level, can vary from school to school, program to program, and state to state. A good rule of thumb is that, in the case of experiential learning, more is better.

The master's degree has a clinical practicum and internship training component. While the number of required hours per semester or academic year will vary, practicum is usually 100 hours and internship will be a minimum of 600 hours with 40 percent of those hours being direct client/student/consumer contact (Kimbel & Levitt, 2017, p. 34). Typically, a student's work with clients is supervised on a weekly basis by a licensed practitioner. Students may be expected to audio- or videotape client sessions, do informal or formal case presentations, and discuss assigned readings as a part of their supervised experience.

Inherent in a doctoral program is clinical training that is parallel to the educational coursework for the degree. Generally during the second year of a doctoral program, a student will do an assessment practicum in which the student administers, evaluates, and writes reports on psychological assessments under the supervision of a licensed psychologist. The third year of a doctoral program includes the first clinical therapy practicum. That is generally a two-day per week commitment to providing psychotherapy under the clinical supervision of a licensed psychologist. The fourth year includes the advanced clinical therapy practicum, which is generally three days per week. Again, students provide psychotherapy under the clinical supervision of a licensed psychologist. During the fifth year, academic coursework is generally completed. While the other years of training are unpaid, the fifth year is a full-time, paid experience involving a variety of professional responsibilities, including providing psychotherapy, psychological assessment and report writing, outreach, and presentations. Concurrent with these activities, the student is also researching and writing a dissertation.

ACCREDITATION

The foremost national accrediting body for counseling programs in the United States is the Council for Accreditation of Counseling and Related Education Programs (CACREP). CACREP is an independent agency that reviews professional preparation programs within already accredited institutions. It is recognized by the Council for Higher Education Accreditation to accredit master's degree programs in counseling and related education programs. "In order to become accredited, a counselor education program must fulfill certain requirements or standards with regard to institutional settings, program mission and objectives, program content, practicum experiences, student selection and advising, faculty qualifications and workload, program governance, instructional support, and self-evaluation" (http://www.cacrep.org/value-of-accreditation/understanding-accreditation).

The benefits of attending a CACREP-approved program are outlined in their website as

- recognition that the program has been evaluated and meets or exceeds national standards;

- knowledge that the graduate has met prerequisites for credentialing and is ready for entry into professional practice; and

- understanding that the focus of the program will be on professional counseling, not psychology, education or other helping professions (http://www.cacrep.org/home/why-attend-an-accredited-program/).

CERTIFICATIONS

After completion of graduate-level coursework, professional counselors have the option to become a National Certified Counselor (NCC). The National Board of Certified Counselors (NBCC) certification program recognizes counselors who have met predetermined standards in their training, experience, and performance on the National Counselor Examination for Licensure and Certification (NCE), the most portable credentialing examination in counseling. NBCC also offers the following certifications: Certified Mental Health Counselor (CCMHC), Master Addictions Counselor (MAC), and National Certified School Counselor (NCSC) (www.nbcc.org/).

The Commission on Rehabilitation Counselor Certification (CRCC) is an independent, not-for-profit organization dedicated to improving the lives of individuals with disabilities. CRCC sets the standard for quality rehabilitation counseling services through its internationally recognized certification program. Individuals in this specialty often become a Certified Rehabilitation Counselor (http://www.crccertification.com/).

Certifications are completely voluntary and are available for a range of specializations within the profession. Being certified demonstrates to clients, colleagues, and employers that, by meeting the standards of the credentialing organization, you have achieved a high level of professional competence.

LICENSURE

While the American Counseling Association has a licensure policy, it is merely a guideline for the states to consider. Licensure is a credential to practice granted to individuals who have met state-determined standards and policies. In 2016 the ACA published a 168-page document on the licensing requirements of all 50 states, the District of Columbia, and Puerto Rico. It is free to ACA members, and it is useful not only for understanding licensure in your state but also for state-by-state comparisons of educational and continuing education requirements (Shifflett, 2016).

Scope of Practice

"Scope of practice is essentially a phrase used to define the unique nature and focus of a counselor's work. A scope of practice outlines appropriate and inappropriate counseling services and activities that fall within the purview of counselors in specific settings which is based on counselor training, experience, and qualifications. Every State has its own scope of practice for professional counseling that is tied to counselor licensing laws and regulations" (Kimbel & Levitt, 2017, p. 26).

All counselors share a common professional identity in that they are, first and foremost, counselors. Their area of specialization adds another layer to that identity. And finally, the environment in which they operate also further defines their scope of practice. For example, I am a National Certified Counselor (NCC) and a Licensed Clinical Professional Counselor (LCPC) in Illinois. I was also the associate director of a career development center in a university for many years. In that role, I provided career counseling for students and alumni; and I clinically supervised graduate students during their practica and internships. I also provided clinical supervision to the career counselors who were new to the profession and required supervised hours to be licensed. Additionally, I facilitated group supervision for the entire career counseling staff. My scope of practice in that role was determined by the work I did with clients (career counseling) but also by the work I did with staff (clinical supervision).

The Importance of Portability

Licensure portability is defined as "being able to transfer a professional counseling license when a practitioner moves to a different state" ("ACA continues push forward," 2017). For example, being licensed in Illinois will not automatically allow you to practice if you move to California or New York. You may be required to take more courses or to do additional supervised hours, regardless of the amount of experience you have. This fact has been a constant source of frustration within the profession. In response to this issue, in June 2016 the American Counseling Association's Governing Council passed the Licensure Portability Model:

> A counselor who is licensed at the independent practice level in their home state and who has no disciplinary record shall be eligible for licensure at the independent practice level in any state or U.S. jurisdiction in which they are seeking residence. The state to which the licensed counselor is moving may require a jurisprudence examination based on the rules and procedures of that state. (https://www.counseling.org/knowledge-center/licensure-requirements/licensure-policies)

You may wonder why a counseling license wasn't always portable. Here's a bit of context that may help you understand why this is an enormous undertaking. While it's hard to believe, it took 33 years for counselors to be licensed in all 50 states. Virginia led the way in 1976; and, in 2009, California was the last state to provide licensure to counselors. In that period of time, the profession grew and changed as did the populations that counselors served. The number of hours of coursework and supervised training increased over time. The specific set of courses required in 1980 was not the same as courses required in 2015. And all of these requirements were different from state to state ("ACA continues push forward," 2017).

In 2015 ACA asked all state licensing boards to adopt a uniform professional title, Licensed Professional Counselor (LPC), and offered a five-paragraph job description that delineated the work of LPCs (Bray, 2015). Most state boards already require 60 hours of coursework and 3,000 hours of post-master's supervision, and the profession, through accreditation, has worked toward standardization. Licensure is granted by the states, and each state board will ultimately have to agree to portability. Since it took 33 years for licensure to be a reality in the United States, portability may be a long time coming. (Think 13 colonies becoming one country!) However, the good news is that the process has begun.

References

ACA continues push forward for licensure portability. (2017, June 6). *Counseling Today*. Retrieved from https://ct.counseling.org/2017/06/aca-continues-push-forward-licensure-portability/

Bray, B. (2015, July 20). State licensing boards asked to adopt uniform scope of practice, licensure title. *Counseling Today*. Retrieved from https://ct.counseling.org/2015/07/state-licensing-boards-asked-to-adopt-uniform-scope-of-practice-licensure-title

Buffardi, L. E. (2010, November 10). Knowing is half the battle (part 1): What type of graduate program should you apply to? *Psychology Today*. Retrieved from https://www.psychologytoday.com/blog/grad-school-guru/201011/knowing-is-half-the-battle-part-1

Kimbel, T. M., & Levitt, D. H. (2017). *A guide to graduate programs in counseling*. New York, NY: Oxford University Press.

Shifflett, E. T. (Ed.). (2016). *Licensure requirements for professional counselors – 2016*. Alexandria, VA: American Counseling Association.

3

ADDICTION COUNSELORS

A DAY IN THE LIFE

The ACA Encyclopedia of Counseling defines addiction as "a preoccupation with and a dependence on a drug or process, resulting in increased tolerance, withdrawal and repeated patterns of relapse" (Valente, 2009, p. 4). As an addiction counselor, you will guide people who have substance addictions, like alcohol or legal and/ or illegal drugs. These substances are consumed to alter the user's functioning or level of consciousness for the purposes of increasing pleasure, diminishing physical or psychic pain, enhancing relaxation, stimulation, or social interactions. You are also likely to serve people who have process addictions, that is, eating disorders, pornography, gambling, sex, shopping, surfing the Internet. Process addictions are behavioral compulsions and, like substance addictions, alter consciousness. Any addiction impairs the user's ability to function effectively with friends and family, or adequately manage their financial, legal, or vocational lives.

You would provide treatment and support both one-on-one and in group sessions to help clients recover from addiction or modify problem behaviors. "Addiction counselors provide education about the nature and progression of addiction; teach relapse prevention strategies, encourage coping skills; and, in the process, use a variety of counseling techniques to bring about change. . . . Addiction counselors can be viewed as teachers, coaches, or advocates, depending on the stage of the client's treatment" (Valente 2009, p. 5).

You may encourage your clients to participate in 12-step programs as well as incorporate program principles into your practice. You may also help clients rebuild personal relationships by working directly with your clients and their families. When necessary, you will counsel your clients in re-establishing professional relationships and their careers.

You may work as part of a team of medical and mental health professionals in a behavioral counseling center, hospital, residential treatment facility, intensive outpatient program, half-way house, correctional facility, or other clinical settings. Group and individual counseling for addiction is also provided in community agencies and private practice offices.

Addiction counselors must have a range of interpersonal skills including empathy, cultural sensitivity, consistency, the ability to set and maintain boundaries, and a belief in your clients' capacity for change and growth.

To sum it up, as an addiction counselor you will

- counsel clients, individually or in group sessions, to assist in overcoming dependencies, adjusting to life, or making changes;

- participate in case conferences or staff meetings and may be required to report to a court about a client's treatment and progress;

- assist clients in connecting with needed community resources, including 12-step programs, medical professionals, and agencies that can provide a range of services including housing, employment, family and general case management; and

- be responsible for keeping detailed records for each client including histories, treatment plans and progress, services provided (Bureau of Labor Statistics [BLS], 2017).

SALARY AND JOB OUTLOOK

Currently, the median salary for addiction counselors is $42,150, with top salaries in the $65,000 range. As of 2016, there were approximately 102,400 addiction counselors working in a variety of industries. The field of addiction counseling has a projected higher than average growth rate of 20 percent through 2026 (BLS, 2017).

According to the Bureau of Labor Statistics (2017), average salaries in the industries with the highest level of employment in this occupation are:

- Hospitals, state, local, and private $48,300

- State and local government, excluding education and hospitals $45,990

- Outpatient care centers $39,820

- Individual and family services $39,130

- Residential, mental health, and substance abuse facilities $37,050

Other industries that employ addiction counselors include colleges and universities, elementary and secondary schools, offices of other health care practitioners, other residential facilities, vocational rehabilitation, adult and juvenile offender rehabilitation, and private practice.

BEST PREPARATION

While the field of addiction employs individuals with all levels of education, those with a master's degree are able to provide comprehensive services to their clients, including individual and group counseling.

Addiction counseling master's programs prepare graduates to work with persons and families affected by alcohol, drugs, gambling, sexual, and other addictive disorders (e.g., food related). These 60-semester-hour programs focus on models of treatment, prevention, recovery, and relapse prevention, along with the appropriate application of interventions. Graduates of addiction counseling programs may choose to work in private practice or may work in a variety of community agencies offering counseling services for substance abuse.

SPECIAL CONSIDERATIONS

The National Certification Commission for Addiction Professionals (NCC AP) has instituted three main credentials for addiction counselors (https://www .naadac.org/certification). Determining which credential is appropriate for you is based on your degree of knowledge, education and formal training, and your skillset. Movement through the credentials is possible.

- National Certified Addiction Counselor, Level I (NCAC I)

- National Certified Addiction Counselor, Level II (NCAC II)

- Master Addiction Counselor with Co-Occurring Disorders Component (MAC)

The NCC AP also offers opportunities for specialization credentials and endorsements:

- Nicotine Dependence Specialist (NDS)

- National Certified Adolescent Addiction Counselor (NCAAC)

- National Endorsed Student Assistance Professional (NESAP)

- National Clinical Supervision Endorsement (NCSE)

- National Endorsed Co-Occurring Disorders Professional (NECODP)

- National Peer Recovery Support Specialist (NCPRSS)

For an explanation of each of these credentials, please see: https://www.naadac .org/assets/2416/nccap_credentials_flyer_may2016.pdf.

The American Mental Health Counselors Association also offers the AMHCA Diplomate, Specialist in Substance Abuse and Co-occurring Disorders Counseling. For an explanation of this credential, please see http://connections.amhca .org/Go.aspx?MicrositeGroupTypeRouteDesignKey=430fca37-b93a-492b-8d69-277eef72bd9b&NavigationKey=500571de-6d00-4219-869f-8e5b75311535.

And finally, "One characteristic found among many addiction counselors is previous personal or familial experience with addiction. As a result, addiction counselors are encouraged to have a least one year or more of sobriety prior to engaging in addiction counseling" (Valente 2009, p. 5).

ADDITIONAL RESOURCES

Addiction Technology Transfer Center Network	http://www.nattc.org/
American Counseling Association	https://www.counseling.org/
American Mental Health Counselors Association	http://www.amhca.org/
International Association of Addictions and Offender Counselors (IAAOC)	http://www.iaaoc.org/
NAADAC (National Association for Alcoholism and Drug Abuse Counselors), the Association for Addiction Professionals	https://www.naadac.org/

MEET SERENA WADHWA, PSYD, LCPC, CADC, RYT

What has your career trajectory been? What prompted your decision to become an addiction counselor?

It really began in undergrad, when I was unable to understand how a drug can be more powerful than a relationship. At the time, I knew nothing about substance use disorders and when I moved back home for various reasons, I decided to take an Intro to Addictions course at the local community college. I then realized this was my path. There is more to this story of course, and I share it when I do trainings or teach about substance use disorders

What is your current job and professional title? How long have you been doing this type of work?

Currently, I am an assistant professor and program coordinator. I oversee an addiction counseling program where students who complete the 60 credit-hour program are then eligible to take their CADC exam and apply for the LPC exam. I have been at the university for about seven years. I've been a clinical therapist for about 10 years and have worked in the field of substance use disorders for about 20 years. I currently am also an author, a blogger, a yoga instructor, a stress coach, and a podcast host.

Please describe the environment(s) you work in. What are some of the pros and cons of the environment(s)?

I work in a university setting, and we have a great department. My chair is very supportive of the team's individual strengths, and that is what contributes to how well we have worked together and contributed to various projects.

At the hospital outpatient practice I am at, again, the environment is amazing. When I have worked at a treatment setting, there has also been this teamwork approach and professional development has been a top priority. Sometimes the stress can be overwhelming, which is why having a self-care routine is important.

Please describe a typical day/week at your job.

Well, it depends on the day. I can be in meetings, grading, facilitating a group, meeting with students in my program, finding current information to disseminate, writing. Every day is different.

What are the best and worst parts of your job and profession?

Since I am on a tenure track, sometimes it can be overwhelming with the service and research/creative activities. Again, because we have inclusive criteria, it gives some space to do what we are good at. I love teaching the next generation of counselors, sharing what I have learned and the evidence-based practices, staying current and really flourishing in professional development. I love working with others to help them enhance their lives, whether it's by education, learning new skills or tools, or helping them heal.

What would have been helpful to know when you first embarked upon this career?

Initially, I was a CADC and had an MA. Once I decided to pursue my licensure (LPC then LCPC) it really opened up a lot of doors. Once I completed my doctorate, more doors opened. Knowing the different paths that exist and what one can do with different certifications and licensures is something I provide my students with so that they don't box themselves in as I initially did.

What should individuals exploring this career consider in order to make the best decision?

Figure out what your passion is and how you want to bring that out to the world. If you see people doing what you want to do, ask them about it. Get different perspectives. We tend to get stuck in our own way of thinking sometimes, and listening to other perspectives about their career choices, paths, and opportunities can be helpful.

What is the best preparation for individuals considering this field?

Make sure you have a self-care routine. It's easy to burn out (one of the reasons stress became a passion of mine). Set boundaries. Figure out where your heart and soul lie because that is the start of your path. When you love what you do, it isn't work, right? So find creative ways to bring the best you to the field, because substance use disorders are hard and painful. When people heal, that is rewarding.

Final thoughts . . . anything else that would be important to know about this work?

Be curious and know you do make a difference.

(S. Wadhwa, personal communication, September 27, 2017)

References

Bureau of Labor Statistics, U.S. Department of Labor. (2017). Substance abuse, behavioral disorder, and mental health counselors. *Occupational outlook handbook.* Retrieved from https://www.bls.gov/ooh/community-and-social-service/substance-abuse-behavioral-disorder-and-mental-health-counselors.htm

Valente, S. I. (2009). Addiction counseling. In *The ACA encyclopedia of counseling* (pp. 4–7). Alexandria, VA: American Counseling Association.

CAREER COUNSELORS

A DAY IN THE LIFE

As a career counselor, you will spend your day helping clients clarify their career interests, hone in on their career goals, and find effective solutions to the challenges they face as they choose and pursue a career path. Many career counselors work with students in secondary education or college and university settings. Career counselors in higher education may find their clientele includes alumni or community members. Some career counselors work in firms, government or community agencies advising career changers, or assisting laid-off workers in their transition to a new job or career. Others work in corporate career centers where they assist employees in determining their professional goals and identifying company pathways to those goals.

In some cases, you will use aptitude and achievement assessments to help clients identify and evaluate their values, interests, skills, and abilities. Because their careers must fit into the lives they wish to lead, you will also help clients explore the impact of their background (i.e., family, gender, culture, economic status, geography), education, and experience, as these are some of the key factors affecting your clients' career choices and their ability to develop achievable goals. Creating career goals also requires research on career requirements, the realities of working in a particular profession, and an understanding of market trends. Career counselors must be able to access this information and teach clients to do the same. Helping clients master job search skills, such as resume writing, interviewing, and networking—both online and in person, is often a critical part of a career counselor's job.

You may also advise clients on how to resolve problems in the workplace. Some of these problems will be specific to the employer (e.g., understaffing, changes in management or mission) and some will belong to the client (e.g., difficulty with authority, teamwork, or communication). When a client seems to encounter the same issues or intense emotions in every job, it's a telltale sign that work conflicts stem from replaying family of origin roles (Jacobsen, 1999). You may find your work with a client includes bringing to light the connection between their reactions and family of origin issues and helping them develop more appropriate responses to work situations.

To sum it up, as a career counselor you will

- counsel individuals to help them understand and overcome personal, social, or behavioral problems affecting their vocational situations;

- prepare clients for their vocational choices by encouraging them to explore learning opportunities and to persevere with challenging tasks;

- evaluate individuals' abilities, interests, and personality characteristics using tests, records, interviews, or professional sources; and

- guide clients in all aspects of occupational research and the job search process.

SALARY AND JOB OUTLOOK

Currently, the median salary for career counselors is $54,560, with top salaries in the $90,030 range. As of 2016, there were approximately 291,700 career counselors working in a variety of industries. (This number does not include those in private practice.) The field of career counseling has a projected higher than average growth rate of 11 percent through 2026 (Bureau of Labor Statistics [BLS], 2017a).

According to the BLS (2017b), salaries in the industries with the highest level of employment in this occupation are:

- College, universities, and professional schools $51,260

- Community colleges $57,340

- Vocational rehabilitation services $39,360

- Individual and family services $44,460

Other industries that employ career counselors include: state and local government, educational support services, technical and trade schools, residential facilities for mental health and substance abuse, employee assistance programs associated with specific industries or organizations, and private practice.

BEST PREPARATION

Career counselors typically have a master's degree in counseling (sometimes with a focus on career) or school counseling. The more exposure you have to different aspects of the world of work, the better prepared you will be for the demands of career counseling. It would be smart to take advantage of the career services offered at your university or alma mater. Participate in workshops, make an appointment with a career counselor, and do some information interviews. Practical experience is always a plus; you can volunteer, do an internship, or get a position with an organization that includes career counseling as a part of its client services. Experience in related fields, like human resources, can also be useful. Finally, consider becoming a mentor. Many organizations, serving a range of populations, offer the opportunity to use your own career expertise to guide people in need of career assistance.

SPECIAL CONSIDERATIONS

The National Career Development Association provides several different certifications. The three listed below are reserved for individuals with counseling degrees (http://ncdacredentialing.org/aws/NCDA/pt/sp/credentials).

- Certified Career Counselor (CCC)—for counselors who will specialize in the delivery of career counseling services

- Certified Clinical Supervisor of Career Counseling (CCSCC)—for individuals who serve as clinical supervisors to career counselors and other practitioners who provide career services

- Certified Career Counselor Educator (CCCE)—for individuals whose primary focus is the training of new counselors who will specialize in the field of career counseling

ADDITIONAL RESOURCES

American Counseling Association	https://www.counseling.org/
National Association of Colleges and Employers (NACE)	www.naceweb.org/
National Career Development Association (NCDA)	www.ncda.org/
National Employment Counseling Association (NECA)	www.employmentcounseling.org/

MEET SUSAN WORTMAN, MED, LCPC

Please describe your career trajectory.

Much of my life, career was not a clear trajectory. As a first-generation college student, I knew higher education was important, but the further engaged I became in academics, the less clear I was on how I would be ready to start a "career" with what I was learning in the classroom. I had always considered myself an English major, before I even knew how college or majors worked, but my sophomore year of college, I started to worry that I didn't know how I would turn my love of analyzing literature into a career (especially as I didn't want to be a teacher). I stumbled into an honors forensic anthropology class and fell deeply in love with the notion of solving puzzles by studying bones and clues in nature, but I felt my scientific acumen was too far removed from my confidence in English Lit, so I settled on what I felt was a natural compromise: psychology.

All through college, I worked in various administrative and educational positions, managing data and mentoring youth in various outdoor topics; both tasks I excelled in but never connected to the concept of what a "career" would entail. I was convinced that my degree in psychology did not qualify me for any specific career, so I would eventually have to attend graduate school to specialize and learn a trade. Looking back, I think part of the problem lay in understanding the differences, but also the connections, between a "career" and a "job." I found myself working a full-time research position with one of my former psychology professors at the university I graduated from, using the stability the job afforded me to both travel and think about what it was I really wanted to do (or in the terms I was currently thinking, "what I would go to graduate school for").

As I reflected over the next few years, I decided that the most meaningful experiences in my life thus far had been mentorship oriented and involved a high level of creativity and autonomy, but also problem solving. I incorporated my interest in psychology and landed on the idea of becoming a high school counselor. Through my counseling graduate program, I was lucky enough to be pushed to complete several informational interviews of individuals currently in the profession I was seeking, which helped me evolve my goal from one engaged in a highly structured high school setting, to one working on a college campus in a career. Now I'm in a profession where I still get to solve puzzles, just not by studying bones and clues in nature. Now my clues are found through the narratives of my clients, and my emphasis and interests in relationships and human behavior are all key elements in helping make these connections clear to others.

What is your job and professional title? How long have you been doing this type of work?

I am a career advisor for Loyola University Chicago's Career Development Center, with my MEd in counseling and my LCPC. I recently started my fifth year in this position, and also completed my clinical internship component at the Center the year before I started full time. Thus far, I'm a one-trick pony, but this has been an amazing environment for fulfilling work.

Please describe the environment you work in. What are some of the pros and cons of the environment?

I work at a large private university in Chicago. My office is host to five full-time career advisors, all with degrees and various levels of licensure in counseling, as well as an associate director who oversees the clinical counseling practicum/internship training and professional development at our site. As a function of this training, we supervise three or four counseling clinical interns each year as they finish their master's degrees and pursue licensure. We operate under a liaison model of advising, where each career advisor focuses his or her time and schedule on developing relationships and resources for specific academic programs. For example, I work primarily with students and alumni in the natural sciences fields, as well as within our School of Nursing programs; lots of health care interests on my plate.

Because we work within a university setting, and because the emphasis on higher education these days has been increasingly job focused, we currently have a good amount of institutional support for the work we do with students. This support, however, also includes some scrutiny and some need to educate-up regarding what we do: we are not a job placement service, nor are we strictly career coaching/didactic in model. Much of what we do is through the lens of identity development and goal discernment and we emphasize the whole-person not just the "job title" or "major" of a student/alum, using our counseling degrees to the fullest. It can be challenging to walk the line between helping students process what is best for them while keeping external and societal expectations and their need to support themselves while juggling student loans in mind. As such, the topic of retention has had a spotlight on it in recent years, and our center operates as a key support for helping students stay in school while they navigate a variety of stressors and factors in their decision-making processes.

Many benefits contribute to a sense of fulfillment for me where I work as well. The team I work on shares a core desire to support our students and each other, and the fact that most of us share a common training in counseling really helps connect our communication and interpersonal styles, despite all having different strengths and approaches. The diversity of our roles and tasks also keeps us busy and on our toes, allowing us to find different tasks that align with our interests. We are never bored!

Please describe a typical day/week at your job.

A typical week usually involves time spent on the following: 10–15 hour individual counseling/advising appointments with students and alumni; teaching (and grading) a three-credit seminar for undergraduate students on career exploration and discernment; corresponding with faculty, staff, and employers to schedule workshops or manage communication about relevant events and information; providing support to various events; providing resume feedback on our database and through e-mail; attending professional development and individual/group supervision pertaining to our counseling degrees; creating customized programming and resources for specific audiences; and the list goes on. Each advisor also has various additional responsibilities depending on their interests, liaison areas, and expertise. For example, I also manage the training and development of our undergraduate career peer advisor program and clinically supervise a graduate student pursuing their master's in counseling. Other advisors manage programming requests, course administration, and alumni mentoring programs. Given the wide range of tasks on our plates, one challenge can be the cognitive switching each day/hour between tasks and the mental energy required to make that shift. As such, it can be important to monitor our schedules and identify what kind of time-management and scheduling strategies are best for us to reach and maintain a state of flow.

What are the best and worst parts of your job and profession?

The best part of my job is that it provides both intrinsic and extrinsic meaning and motivation. Intrinsically, I am able to leverage my strengths and interests in creative problem solving and relationship building, as well as my core values of helping others and continued growth and learning. It is exciting to build a meaningful connection with a person after just one hour of conversation, and to continue that growth and process over a longer period of time, with no limitations by insurance. Extrinsically, I can see and hear the excitement or relief from students as they thank me or move forward to accomplish a goal of theirs. I love getting those e-mails or having a former student drop by with an update on their life—lots of warm fuzzies. I also feel beyond lucky to have landed on such a supportive team, where we all prioritize our students/clients, and practice empathy in all our actions.

The part of my job that I struggle with the most has to be the political side of working in a university. While my focus is primarily turned inward, toward helping my clients and fostering my counseling skills, there are larger cultural and political decisions that my department operates within, and I do not have the autonomy that a private practice clinician would have. That being said, I also really don't enjoy any external networking with employers we have to do . . . maybe it's the introvert in me that doesn't appreciate having to look and perform externally, but as useful as it can be to my job, I still don't relish it.

What would have been helpful to know when you first embarked upon this career?

I think I was lucky to start this career with an eyes-wide-open approach, given the informational interviews I had conducted. However, I don't think I quite realized how unique the counseling-model approach to career advising was at the university I interned at. As I was applying for my first job post-graduation, I had a difficult time identifying career centers that employed/sought licensed counselors and that had the clinical model of advising I was interested in. Hopefully, the profession continues to advocate for this holistic approach through NCDA and ACA and I can continue to advocate for it from my own position now.

What should individuals considering this career consider in order to make the best decision? What is the best preparation for individuals considering this field?

A working knowledge of student affairs in higher education is helpful to understand the general structure (political structure and resources for support) and the student body you'll be working with (a wide range of development here—young adults and older adults, military veterans, non-traditional students, disabled students and alumni, international students, etc.). This also means that a solid foundation and interest in identity issues and multicultural advocacy is crucial. Advising or mentoring experience is critical, and a counseling degree can only further your student-centered approach and effectiveness (a little biased here). Previous work experience in a professional field, so that your knowledge of current career issues (job search, industry trends, and transferable/desired skills) is first-hand and reliable, is also immensely helpful and necessary to be effective. Because careers and industries change so quickly, it is still best to operate on a wide range of knowledge and skills that can apply across academic concentrations, jobs, and industries.

Final thoughts . . . anything else that would be important to know about this work?

Career counseling is still a growing field, especially within a more traditional view of the profession of mental health counseling. As a specialization, it can be an immensely helpful entry-point for clients to start to explore their identities, and can often lead to identification of other mental health concerns that should be addressed. It is also a profession that really lends itself to the professional who enjoys multitasking and flexing a larger set of skills: from teaching and presenting, to group facilitation, to resource building, and the occasional event management. It also has the capacity to create a blended environment that embraces both the autonomy of clinical work, but also the team environment as we encourage each other to grow professionally through supervision, consultation, and idea generation. There may not be a wide breadth of job opportunities when you look at the different titles a career counselor can embody, but the depth that comes with such varied roles within one profession means a lifetime of continual growth and change and evolution.

(S. Wortman, personal communication, October 4, 2017)

References

Bureau of Labor Statistics, U.S. Department of Labor. (2017a). School and career counselors. *Occupational outlook handbook.* Available at https://www.bls.gov/ooh/community-and-social-service/school-and-career-counselors.htm

Bureau of Labor Statistics, U.S. Department of Labor. (2017b). *Occupational employment statistics, occupational employment and wages, May 2016.* Retrieved from https://www.bls.gov/oes/current/oes211012.htm

Jacobsen, M. H. (1999). *Hand-me-down dreams: How families influence our career paths & how we can reclaim them* (pp. 122–132). New York, NY: Three Rivers Press.

5

CHILD AND ADOLESCENT COUNSELORS

A DAY IN THE LIFE

Growing up is a challenging process. When life is going relatively well—not only for the child or adolescent but also for the whole family, community, and culture—most individuals can master developmental challenges and reach adulthood reasonably unscathed. However, on any given day or in any given lifetime, all children and adolescents must handle and become proficient at normal developmental tasks; many face a range of adverse experiences as well. A child's or adolescent's ability to function successfully is influenced by a myriad of factors including social influences of parents and family as well as peers; biological, cognitive, social, and emotional changes; culture, race, and economic class; religion; and gender identity and sexual identity.

Between 1995 and 1997, the Adverse Childhood Experiences (ACE), a collaborative project between Kaiser Permanente and the Centers for Disease Control and Prevention that studied over 17,000 ordinary Americans, presented evidence for relationships between adverse childhood experiences, household dysfunction, and negative health outcomes during childhood and later in life. This "biography becomes biology" perspective has generated a raft of research, the results of which have both underscored and elaborated upon the original findings. ACE identified categories of adversity: physical abuse, sexual abuse, emotional abuse, physical neglect, emotional neglect, violent treatment of mother, loss of a parent for any reason, mental illness in the house including suicidal behavior and institutionalization, substance abuse in the house, and criminal behavior in the home including incarceration of a household member. "We are coming to understand that, when dealing specifically with children, a wider range of traumatic experiences can be equally devastating and produce debilitating outcomes years later. Further studies are also uncovering negative outcomes related to more 'ordinary' adversities such as accidents, childhood hospitalizations or the loss of a sibling" (Morgan, 2017, p. 50). Trauma science has gone on to support the ACE results that suggest that different categories of adversity were about equal in the damage they caused.

Enter child and adolescent counselors—individuals who have elected to work with these populations through the experiences of normal development, adversity, and trauma. As a child and adolescent counselor, you must be grounded in counseling theory that is effective for the populations you serve and the issues they face. Systems approaches and the theoretical perspectives and techniques provided by cognitive-behavioral, Adlerian, solution-focused, and integrative theories can all prove useful depending on the child's or adolescent's concerns and needs. You are likely to provide individual and family therapy, and play therapy, and may facilitate psycho-educational as well as counseling groups for children, adolescents, parents, and families. Your work could take place in a range of environments including schools, community and government agencies, residential treatment facilities, hospitals, and private practice.

To sum it up, as a child and adolescent counselor you will

- assess, evaluate, and counsel children and adolescents utilizing developmentally appropriate prevention and intervention strategies;

- assess, evaluate, and counsel children and adolescents with special needs utilizing developmentally appropriate prevention and intervention strategies;

- provide crisis intervention services as required;

- deliver counseling and education for parents and families of children and adolescents;

- consult with caretakers and other professionals who are involved in the lives of children and adolescents; and

- create awareness of child and adolescent mental health issues and advocate for improvement within the profession and the community.

SALARY AND JOB OUTLOOK*

Currently, the median salary for mental health counselors is $42,840, with top salaries in the $70,100 range. As of 2016, there were approximately 157,700 mental health counselors working in a variety of industries. The field has a projected higher than average growth rate of 20 percent through 2026 (Bureau of Labor Statistics [BLS], 2017).

According to the BSL (2017), salaries in the industries with the highest level of employment in this occupation are:

- State and local government, excluding education and hospitals $50,840
- Hospitals; state, local, and private $46,390
- Individual and family services $41,720
- Outpatient mental health and substance abuse centers $41,650
- Residential facilities $36,800

Other industries that employ child and adolescent counselors include educational support services, offices of other health care practitioners, community social service agencies, and private practice.

BEST PREPARATION

In addition to choosing a master's degree in counseling or a related field, seek out opportunities to work with children and adolescents. Volunteer or find employment in organizations that serve these populations. Experience is your best guide in determining the type of client (age, needs, focus of your work with them, etc.) you're interested in serving, the issues you want to immerse yourself in when working with children and adolescents, and the types of skills and mind-set required to be an effective child and adolescent counselor.

*Statistics for mental health counselors are used because salary and job outlook is not available for the specialty of child and adolescent counseling.

SPECIAL CONSIDERATIONS

- AMHCA Diplomate, Specialist in Child and Adolescent Counseling—establishes a clinical mental health counselor standard in treating child or adolescent issues, and augments the credibility of clinical mental health treatment for this population. Candidates are required to be knowledgeable with the distinctive ethics and standards of practice in the treatment of children and adolescents. (http://connections .amhca.org/Go.aspx?MicrositeGroupTypeRouteDesignKey=430 fca37-b93a-492b-8d69-277eef72bd9b&NavigationKey=23afeb9d-0b89-4458-9766-f8d3cef81882)

Federal and state statutes as well as the counseling profession itself affect the work of professional counselors. Counselors, regardless of specialty, are required in all 50 states and Washington, DC, to report suspected child abuse or neglect to the proper authorities. In these cases, counselors are immune from any civil or criminal liability for breaking confidentiality.

However, child and adolescent counselors in community or private practice settings must sometimes adhere to a different standard than school counselors. While children and adolescents in school settings have a right to voluntary counseling without parental consent, "In community counseling, minors must have consent from a parent or guardian or a court order to receive counseling services. . . . Informing parents and/or guardians about the purpose of counseling and the limits of confidentiality is an ethical obligation of counselors when working with minors in any context" (Leggett, 2009, p. 414).

ADDITIONAL RESOURCES

American Counseling Association	https://www.counseling.org/
American Mental Health Counselors Association (AMHCA)	http://www.amhca.org/
Association for Child and Adolescent Counseling (ACAC)	http://acachild.org/

MEET DIANE MCDONALD, MED, LCPC

What has your career trajectory been? What prompted your decision to become a child and adolescent counselor?

I began my career as a counselor 28 years ago. I have gone from working at an inpatient residential treatment center to working on a grant to integrate children back from residential treatment to supporting schools to improve programs for children with mental health challenges to private practice work. I have been a therapist, coach, facilitator, coordinator, consultant, and trainer throughout my career. Below is a detailed overview of my career:

- Counselor in a college setting—Personal and career counseling

- Therapist—Child and adolescent residential treatment (2 years)

- Reintegration specialist—Grant project for state education system; worked with schools to reintegrate students back from residential treatment into their home communities by developing school, home, and community plans.

- Family services facilitator—Special education coop; worked with students with emotional and behavior disabilities and their families. Developed comprehensive home, school, and community plans to improve quality of life for students and their families (5 years)

- Technical assistance coach—Grant project for state education system; supported school districts in the implementation of Tier 2 and 3 behavior supports for students. Trainer for mental health first aid, wraparound, and trauma.

- Therapist—Private practice (5 years)

I decided to go into counseling during my last year of college. I originally thought that I would be a high school counselor. I began volunteering as a guide for wilderness trips in Canada, where I worked with high school students. I discovered that I loved working with teens. As a graduate student in my counseling program I also became aware of how important it is to include parents and caregivers in the treatment of children and adolescents. I realized that it would be challenging for me to work within a school setting where my contact with families would be limited.

What is your current job and professional title? How long have you been doing this type of work?

I have two jobs currently. As a licensed clinical professional counselor, I see clients, school-age through adult, in a private practice setting. I have been doing this part time for five years. As a technical assistance coach, I work for a state education department. I have been doing this work for 20 years. My primary focus has been improving outcomes for students K–12 who have emotional and behavioral challenges. In this role I have supported schools with developing comprehensive plans for students and their families through a process called wraparound. I have been a wraparound facilitator, coach, and trainer for school districts. I have also supported schools with the implementation of trauma-informed practices in the classroom, positive behavior supports, and mental health first aid.

Please describe the environment(s) you work in. What are some of the pros and cons of the environment(s)?

Private practice: I have a small office where I practice as a sole practitioner.

Pros: Flexible hours and autonomy

Cons: Limited access to colleagues (I love working with a team and do not get that in a solo practice.)

Technical assistance coach: Home office and various school districts across a region of the state

Pros: I love working with dedicated school professionals who have a passion to improve quality of life for children and families. It has also been rewarding to be involved in developing programs for children and families.

Cons: Entails a lot of travel. It makes juggling a family life and a private practice difficult.

Please describe a typical day/week at your job.

Private practice:

Because I do this work part time, I conduct most of my full-time job during the day. I schedule clients during late afternoon hours and evenings. I also see clients on the weekends. As a child/adolescent counselor it is important to have late afternoon and evening appointments to accommodate school schedules. On some days I may find myself contacting parents, school personnel, and insurance companies.

Technical assistance coach:

Conference calls with my team. I may travel 3–4 days per week to meet with school teams to provide coaching support. Some days I may be providing training for multiple school districts.

What are the best and worst parts of your job and profession?

Best parts of my profession: I have been able to work within multiple settings over the course of my career, from inpatient residential settings, school settings, and private practice settings. My focus has always been to develop ways to improve the quality of life for children and families who struggle with mental health challenges, and I am constantly learning and changing how I do this work.

Worst parts of the job: It can be challenging to make time for self-care and family. Working with children and adolescents requires a commitment to working afternoons and evenings. This can be challenging when raising your own children. It is one reason I delayed my private practice work for later in my career.

What would have been helpful to know when you first embarked upon this career?

A counseling degree is quite flexible. Persons with this degree can do many types of careers beyond traditional psychotherapist. It would have also been helpful to know about the business aspects of private practice. I have discovered that counselors do not always have the business skills to develop a thriving private practice. Preparation for this is critical for those wanting to be owners of their own business.

What should individuals exploring this career consider in order to make the best decision?

When working with children and adolescents consider that you will also be working with the systems where a child and adolescent exist—family, school, and community. To be effective, the child and adolescent counselor must also be able to work as a team member with individuals from the other systems in a child's life. The child and adolescent counselor must be able to effectively support families and view them from a strength-based perspective.

What is the best preparation for individuals considering this field?

The more experience one has working in multiple settings (hospital, community agency, school, etc.) the easier it will be to work with the many systems that touch a child's life.

Final thoughts . . . anything else that would be important to know about this work?

Find a mentor. Build a network with other professionals where you can encourage and support each other.

(D. McDonald, personal communication, October 16, 2017)

References

Bureau of Labor Statistics, U.S. Department of Labor. (2017). Substance abuse, behavioral disorder, and mental health counselors. *Occupational outlook handbook.* Retrieved from https://www.bls.gov/ooh/community-and-social-service/substance-abuse-behavioral-disorder-and-mental-health-counselors.htm

Leggett, E. S. (2009). Professional identity and ethics, key legal issues in counseling minors (p. 414). *The ACA encyclopedia of counseling.* Alexandria, VA: American Counseling Association.

Morgan, O. J. (2017, September). Coming to grips with childhood adversity. *Counseling Today, 60*(3), 48–53.

6

CLINICAL MENTAL
HEALTH COUNSELORS

A DAY IN THE LIFE

Counseling with an emphasis on human development across the life span, prevention, and wellness is the purview of clinical mental health counselors. Your work with individuals and groups can address a spectrum of mental and emotional disorders; however, your focus remains understanding client behaviors and specific events within the context of their lived experience in order to promote the mental and emotional health of the people you serve. In order to do so, you may choose to support individuals dealing with issues associated with addictions and substance abuse; family, parenting, and marital problems; physical health concerns; stress management; self-esteem; aging; depression and anxiety; grief and loss; trauma; and psychopathology. Through education and counseling, you guide your clients in identifying their strengths and resources as they learn to manage their concerns more effectively and live more fulfilling lives.

You may work alone, counseling individuals, couples, families, or groups, or you may work as part of a group practice or an interdisciplinary team, collaborating with physicians, social workers, health educators, and others to treat illness and promote overall wellness. Clinical mental health counselors work in a variety of settings including community-based mental health centers, hospitals and other treatment centers, education, government agencies, residential treatment facilities, prisons, or employee assistance organizations.

To sum it up, as a clinical mental health counselor you will

- collect information about individuals or clients, using interviews, case histories, observational techniques, and other assessment methods;

- counsel individuals, families, or groups to help them understand problems, deal with crisis situations, define goals, develop realistic action plans in order to effectively manage transitions and achieve personal, social, educational, or vocational developmental milestones;

- diagnose psychopathology and develop and execute treatment plans based on clients' abilities and needs; and

- document patient information including session notes, progress notes, referrals, and recommendations.

SALARY AND JOB OUTLOOK

In order to be inclusive in this very broad category, we will look at the BLS information for both mental health counselors and counseling psychologists. While educational differences account for variations in salary and job outlook, it is important to recognize that master's-prepared counselors with experience and/or certifications will increase their income as well as the demand for their services.

Currently, the median salary for mental health counselors is $42,840, with top salaries in the $70,100 range. As of 2016, there were approximately 157,700 mental health counselors working in a variety of industries. The field has a projected higher than average growth rate of 20 percent through 2026 (Bureau of Labor Statistics [BLS], 2017a). Please see Chapter 5 for a list of industries with the highest employment levels for mental health counselors.

The average salary for counseling psychologists is $73,270, with top salaries reaching $121,610 annually. As of 2016, there were approximately 147,500 counseling psychologists working in a variety of industries. This occupation also has a projected growth rate of 14 percent (BSL, 2017b).

Elementary, secondary and higher education, and private practice provide the greatest number of jobs for counseling psychologists.

BEST PREPARATION

Clinical mental health counseling attracts a range of practitioners in terms of education, focus of experience, and the types of environments that offer employment. To that end, it is critical to use information interviews, field research, volunteer involvement, and work experience to help you determine the specifics of the work you want to do including the populations you are most interested in working with, the environments that best suit your clinical approach and worldview, and the educational preparation (master's or PhD in counseling psychology) that will best suit your aspirations.

SPECIAL CONSIDERATIONS

The National Board of Certified Counselors offers the following certifications:

- National Certified Counselor (NCC) (http://www.nbcc.org/Certification/NCC)

- Certified Clinical Mental Health Counselor (CCMHC) (http://www.nbcc.org/Certification/SpecialtyCertifications)

The American Mental Health Counselors Association is the first association to recognize both advanced practice and professional expertise in clinical mental health counseling. The term "clinical mental health counselor" applies to all individuals licensed to practice clinical counseling regardless of their official state title (http://www.amhca.org/career/diplomate).

- AMHCA Diplomate and Clinical Mental Health Specialist

- AMHCA Diplomate, Specialist in Trauma Counseling

ADDITIONAL RESOURCES

American Counseling Association	https://www.counseling.org/
American Mental Health Counselors Association	http://www.amhca.org/home

MEET THE EXPERTS

Because of the breadth and depth of this arena of counseling, two practitioners have offered their views on the field. They are different in terms of their background, education, and vocational focus and will provide you with a sense of the scope of the work of a clinical mental health counselor.

Meet Kenneth Jackson, PhD, HSPP, NCC

What has your career trajectory been? What prompted your decision to become a counselor?

I was the first in my family to go to college and had to learn to navigate it on my own. I began my freshman year of college at the Art Institute of Pittsburgh in the commercial art program. Realizing this course of study was not for me, I withdrew from school. The following fall I went to a liberal arts college, pursuing a fine arts major with an education degree. I also enrolled in numerous psychology courses.

After college and an unsuccessful search for teaching positions, I enrolled in a training program for cosmetology. In my work as a cosmetologist on Chicago's Northshore, I specialized in color and design. All day I encountered people with interesting life stories; some that included life dilemmas. As the years of work continued, I developed interpersonal confidence and competence and became a skilled tertiary helper; but I wanted to become more proficient. I discovered the emerging field of counseling and enrolled at Northeastern Illinois University's master's in counseling program, one of the first CACREP-accredited programs in the area. My clinical internship was at an inpatient hospital program for substance abuse. I found it challenging but also rewarding, and my desire to apply to PhD programs grew.

I became a student at large in the counseling psychology program at Loyola University Chicago. In a side conversation with my mentor, he encouraged me to apply for the doctoral program. The serendipity of the situation remains cornerstone to my current profession. I explained that I had applied, but I had not heard anything back. On the face of it, my candidacy was not as competitive as other applicants; however, the professor encouraged the selection committee to at least meet me. Of the nearly 300 applicants, 15 were selected for on-site interviews, which included a presentation of research interests. Five applicants made up that year's cohort, and I was very fortunate to receive an offer, which I accepted with immense gratitude.

My exposure to an expanding diversity of clients was cornerstone to my training experience. My clinical experience during my PhD program included a cooperative site providing counseling services at an outpatient methadone clinic for probation/parole clients, career counseling for students and alumni at Loyola's Career Center, and inpatient hospital work with adolescents and with substance abuse. My final clinical internship was at a north suburban Department of Health and Human Service. The training included psychological assessment and outpatient community mental health services. I worked with adolescents and adults across the life span on various mental health concerns including depression, anxiety, substance abuse, and academic challenges related to learning disorders and/or ADHD. The site also provided couples and family therapy and community outreach.

Upon graduation, I began working on securing my post-doctoral training and hours for licensure at a community mental health agency. Later, I secured a job with Chicago Public Schools as a school counselor. I worked in that position as I also developed a private practice. While I was working as a school counselor, I secured my administrators' certification in Illinois and left Chicago Public Schools for a suburban high school district.

Given my background in education, clinical training, administrative credentials, and licenses, I next applied for and was offered the position of director of counseling at Purdue University Calumet in Hammond, Indiana.

What is your current job and professional title? How long have you been doing this type of work?

My job title is executive director of the counseling center at Purdue University Northwest. I have been in this role for 11 years. My primary role is first and foremost as a psychologist providing clinical mental health services, supervision of outreach services, and structure of office function with regard to caseload of clinicians. I also supervise staff psychologists, doctoral externs and a post-doctoral trainee, and the Disability Access Center director. Additionally, I serve as a member of the Behavior Intervention Team (BIT) in a consultant role pertaining to students who exhibit threatening behavior to the campus community. My role also includes consulting with residential housing professionals; working closely with the conduct officer, dean of students, and faculty regarding specific students of concern; and providing training on various topics based on faculty request.

Over the years of being in the job, I have established an awareness of the need for data and designed systems for gathering data that are useful in developing and evaluating programs and services, creating annual reports, and sustaining funding for the effectiveness of the counseling center.

Please describe the environment you work in. What are some of the pros and cons of the environment?

The work environment is a separate and private office location for the Counseling Center that provides a measure of confidentiality to our students who use the on-campus counseling services. The office is "off the beaten path" and thus is somewhat separated from other student services offices. The work is largely one on one with student clients and can contribute to a sense of and experience of isolation from colleagues given that we work primarily with students and behind closed doors. The day is structured with any perceived "down time" allocated to doing clinical notes, which involves more sitting at a computer keyboard.

Please describe a typical day/week at your job.

There really is no typical day on the job—except to say that it is always variable. Of course, there are scheduled appointments, meetings, and trainings but there are also almost always unexpected things that occur that may pull me away from planned activities. We provide crisis walk-in service for students, and there are occasions when we also have a student who expresses suicidal ideation and we must respond immediately.

What are the best and worst parts of your job and profession?

The best part of the job is working with students, both those who are enrolled as students at the university and those doctoral practicum externs from doctoral programs from Chicago-area universities and professional schools of psychology. I also work with some great professionals in my office and across the university who are colleagues and friends. I can rely upon them for their professional perspective and direction on various topics and/or initiatives.

Another great aspect of the job is working with early career psychologists (doctoral students) each year. Our selected trainees have been men and women who are African American, Caucasian, Asian, South Asian, straight and LGBT, and international students. The diversity of race and culture expands our experiences as a group, and the early careerist brings new and exciting perspectives of what is going on in research and training in psychology.

Perhaps the most challenging aspect of the job is that the university is located in a National Shortage area for mental health. Many of our students come with mental health concerns that have never been identified or treated. Additionally, many students may have unidentified disabilities that make the demands of independent learning difficult. Often, our students do not have insurance or the financial resources to access medical care.

Shrinking budgets is another area that is challenging in that there has been a documented increase in demand and severity of mental health concerns on college campuses.

What would have been helpful to know when you first embarked upon this career?

I am doing what I have trained to do in terms of my professional role as a psychologist. The challenges are from the administrative aspects of the job. Things in higher education have become increasingly more complex in the years that I have been working at the university.

What should individuals exploring this career consider in order to make the best decision?

Do the research to understand the education and professional commitment becoming a counseling psychologist requires. The doctoral degree in psychology is the entry into the profession. There is another hurdle to clear, however, to function as an independent psychologist: one year of post-doctoral work under the supervision of a licensed psychologist. Once that year of post-doctoral training is complete, one is eligible to apply for the EPPP licensing exam to become a licensed psychologist. Once licensed, one can begin to work independently (without the clinical supervision of a licensed psychologist).

What is the best preparation for individuals considering this field?

If someone is interested in working in higher education at a college/university counseling center, it is best to do clinical training practicum, the full-time internship year, and/or post-doctoral training working in a college/university counseling center. With specialized work in a college/university counseling center, one can become a viable candidate for employment in higher education. It is noteworthy that working in higher education is often not as highly paid as in a private group practice.

I opted to develop a private practice as well (nights and Saturdays). It provides a different focus of practice (for me, I see high-functioning adults across the life span), which I enjoy. A private practice requires a license and a source of income to pay the initial bills. One usually starts by office share in other practice spaces. If you join a private practice, it's helpful to have an attorney review the contract, particularly if it has a "no compete" clause that may limit your location options if you open your own practice later.

In a private practice, the ability to bill insurance for services is essential. You will need to have the psychologist license, malpractice insurance, an EIN (Employer Identification Number, for business tax purposes), and an NPI number (national provider). The application review process to become credentialed with insurance companies may take 90–180 days. You will need business development skills to market and promote your business to potential clients. Collaborating with other professionals through professional and community organizations is a very helpful tool in developing a private practice. Becoming familiar with psychiatrists to whom you can refer is also beneficial in that you may receive some referrals from the psychiatrist for clients seeking and/or interested in psychotherapy in conjunction with a psychotropic medication treatment approach.

(K. Jackson, personal communication, September 15, 2017)

Meet Cindy Montgomery, MEd, LPCC

What has your career trajectory been? What prompted your decision to become a counselor?

Growing up in a family of educators, I always knew that I wanted to become a teacher. I loved learning, and school was like a second home for me. I graduated from college with a degree in Liberal Studies, which focused on K–12 education. However, at some point during those four years, I realized that I did not want to be confined to the four walls of a classroom. Instead of teaching, I chose to work in higher education, where I instructed students, faculty, and staff on issues of diversity and broadened their global worldview through cultural immersion experiences abroad.

Upon returning stateside, I spent time evaluating my work experiences and what I enjoyed the most. It was the opportunity it afforded me to talk with individuals one-on-one, to hear their stories, and offer encouragement, support, or advice. I pursued a degree in counseling, so that I was better equipped and qualified to assist students who were going through challenging issues.

Life does not always give you smooth transitions, but I've found that with perseverance, you can get farther than you imagined. I returned to my home state with my master's in counseling, only to be met with licensing challenges. I enrolled in an LPCC Re-specialization certificate program to meet state requirements while once again working in an academic setting. I found myself frequently implementing my counseling skills and knowledge into my daily routine with students. But as life would have it, my family made the choice to move to a new state, which meant new rules and board requirements. I spent time working as a career counselor while pursuing licensure. This further solidified my calling to counsel, and as a result, I chose to leave higher education to pursue counseling in an agency setting.

What is your current job and professional title? How long have you been doing this type of work?

I currently work as a Christian counselor for a faith-based, nonprofit organization that provides a host of resources and services to the community in respective areas across the state. I provide individual, couples, and family counseling to a diverse range of clientele primarily for general mental health issues. I have been working as a counselor in this capacity for a little over a year now.

Please describe the environment(s) you work in. What are some of the pros and cons of the environment(s)?

I serve at two locations in the Phoenix metro area. Both offices are in low-income urban neighborhoods and cater to meeting the needs of individuals and families primarily living on public assistance. We provide clothing, food, parenting support, a pregnancy center, computer assistance, and a resource center. We also offer counseling services, foster care and adoption services, and parent aides.

It was a privilege to start counseling services at our southern office, as this service had not previously been offered at this location. This office functions out of a church, and the individuals who frequent services here are often living at or below the poverty level. Given limited staff and resources, I not only counsel, but I also conduct all the administrative tasks at this location. The need for counseling here is great, however, it is often seen as taboo and/or people have a distorted view of counseling that hinders them from seeking services.

Our central office is located in an actual office building, close to more affluent neighborhoods. As a result, my clientele is more diverse in terms of ethnic and cultural background and socioeconomic status. Although half of my client roster uses a sliding fee scale, I have more clients at our central office who pay the standard rate, which is still much lower than other counseling agencies. I also see EAP [employee assistance program] clients from the organization at this location.

Although there are drawbacks to the environment, I greatly appreciate the spirit of service and the commitment to serving those in need with dignity that is found at both locations.

Please describe a typical day/week at your job.

Typically, I open my calendar to check my schedule, pull client files, review my notes from their last session, and make potential notes for the day's session. I typically see three to six clients on a given work day, spending 45–50 minutes with each one. Post-session activities include scheduling the client's next session and completing progress notes. Occasionally, I may conduct assessments, or spend time researching evidenced-based interventions that may be appropriate for individual clients. Depending on the stage of our counseling relationship, I will also spend time developing counseling goals, treatment planning, and eventually working on their discharge paperwork. When assigned a new client, I collaborate with our administrative assistant to ensure that all billing and intake information is correct. Whenever possible, I review the client's intake packet prior to the start of sessions.

I receive supervision biweekly, and consult with other counselors as needed. Advocacy is also a part of my role, ensuring that my clients receive sufficient sponsorship for necessary services and appropriate referrals.

What are the best and worst parts of your job and profession?

The best part of my profession is the opportunity to walk with clients through difficult seasons of life. It takes a lot of trust and courage to divulge personal matters to a stranger, which is very humbling for me. I count it a great privilege to be invited into the lives of my clients. When they demonstrate in word or action that they trust you, it is the best compliment. I love when I have clients who genuinely want to come each week because they see the value in the work they are doing. I find joy in watching my clients grow, mature, and heal, and in knowing that I am using my gifts and talents to make a positive difference in their lives.

Although I work for a nonprofit organization, the counseling model looks similar to that of a private practice. As counselors, we create our own schedules and determine our availability. As a working mom, I appreciate the flexibility of my job and being able to create a work schedule that supports a healthier work–life balance. Counseling as a profession provides various opportunities and work schedules to meet different lifestyle needs.

The worst part of this profession is wishing you could do more for your clients to help change their situation. Counseling is often used to change the individual, but it may or may not change the situations they face. Given where I work, the need is always great, and counseling does not resolve every situation. Similarly, when clients terminate without communicating, I wonder if there was something more or different I could have done to meet their needs.

What would have been helpful to know when you first embarked upon this career?

It would have been helpful to know the challenges of differing state licensure requirements. When I started my search for graduate programs, I was looking for one that focused more on practice and less on research. I was also looking for a degree that was more general in scope. I was living in California at the time, and the fact that I could not find a counseling program that was not MFT [marriage and family therapy] or a doctoral program did not set off any red flags. Little did I know that my home state was the last to recognize counseling as a licensed profession, and since an LPCC was not offered at the time, neither were graduate programs in this field.

Returning to California, I discovered that they were still developing licensure requirements for an LPCC, which included additional courses not provided by my graduate institution. I have no regrets in attending my alma mater, but it would have been helpful to learn more about the educational and licensing requirements for the state that I intended to reside and practice in prior to making final decisions about graduate school programs.

What should individuals exploring this career consider in order to make the best decision?

When exploring counseling as a career, or any career for that matter, it is important to do your homework. Spend time learning about the different types of counseling positions available in the field, and the different settings that you can work in. Know your own "why" or purpose for entering this profession; what *known* strengths and interests do you possess that may determine your niche in the field. I would also gain an understanding of the similarities and differences between various behavioral health roles—social workers, licensed counselors, psychologists, psychiatrists, and so on. There are many options within the behavioral and mental health fields, so knowing each one allows you to make a more informed decision as to what path best suits you.

What is the best preparation for individuals considering this field?

The educational training that you receive from your graduate degree is paramount to setting a foundation for the counseling profession. It really is an opportunity to learn theory and application, but more importantly, it gives you the space to learn about yourself as an individual and as a future counselor. During my graduate experience, I reflected deeply about who I was (my biases and prejudices, my strengths, and my areas for growth), and who I wanted to be as a counselor. It was a starting point for defining who *I* am as a counselor and what I have to offer to each therapeutic relationship.

Second to knowing who you are and what you bring to the field, I believe exposure will give you the best preparation. Whether you glean it from your internship/practicum experience, or in your first few post-grad counseling positions, it is important to be exposed to a range of mental health issues and individuals.

Final thoughts . . . anything else that would be important to know about this work?

Counseling is not an easy profession. We do not get paid to just sit, listen, and offer advice, but rather to enter the worlds of individuals at critical moments in their lives. We have the pleasure of walking through seasons of life with our clients, while always gauging the appropriate balance in our response. We are delicate, direct, empathic, meticulous, challenging, observant, compassionate, confrontational, open, authentic. As counselors, we courageously embark upon journeys that place our clients as the guide, and where the destination is always a mystery. For me fulfillment comes with being present, sticking it out, and seeing where the journey takes us.

(C. Montgomery, personal communication, September 19, 2017)

References

Bureau of Labor Statistics, U.S. Department of Labor. (2017a). Substance abuse, behavioral disorder, and mental health counselors. *Occupational outlook handbook.* Retrieved from https://www.bls.gov/ooh/community-and-social-service/substance-abuse-behavioral-disorder-and-mental-health-counselors.htm

Bureau of Labor Statistics, U.S. Department of Labor. (2017b). Psychologists. *Occupational outlook handbook.* Retrieved from https://www.bls.gov/ooh/life-physical-and-social-science/psychologists.htm

COUNSELORS AND THE EXPRESSIVE ARTS

A DAY IN THE LIFE

"Expressive arts therapies are defined as the use of art, music, drama, dance/movement, poetry/creative writing, bibliotherapy, play, and sandplay within the context of psychotherapy, counseling, rehabilitation, or medicine. Additionally, expressive therapies are sometimes referred to as 'integrative' when various arts are purposively used in combination in treatment . . . these approaches are "brain-wise" interventions that stimulate whole-brain responses to help individuals of all ages experience reparation, recovery and well-being." (Malchiodi, 2014)

As a counselor using the expressive arts as therapeutic tools, you will use distinct arts-based methods and creative processes for the purpose of improving disability and illness as well as boosting health and wellness. You will typically use these specialized techniques, often in conjunction with talk therapy, to help your clients relax, release their own creativity, and find new and perhaps more comfortable ways to uncover and express their thoughts and feelings—and ultimately gain new insights in a safe environment. Your clients will not be required to have any particular artistic ability. Instead, you will guide them on their senses and allowing their imagination free reign so that they may process creatively in support of their own restoration and recovery. Because each expressive arts modality is distinctive, you will work, within the scope of your own training, to design a plan that employs the best expressive outlet for each client. Outcomes for clients include enriched communication and expression; enhanced physical, emotional, cognitive, and/or social functioning; and advanced growth and healing.

You will find the expressive arts are powerful tools in the treatment of stress, depression, anxiety, attention-deficit hyperactivity, addictions, abuse, trauma, chronic pain, and a range of developmental, medical, and neurological conditions. According to Pehrsson, "the creative arts apply to all developmental stages as well as to clients with special needs. In addition, connecting through creative arts is universal because they apply in one way or another to all cultures; creative arts are multicultural" (Pehrsson, 2009, p. 131). The range of organizations that employ counselors with credentials in one or more of the expressive arts is vast. You may find yourself employed in adult day treatment centers, assisted living facilities and nursing homes, community mental health centers, community residences and halfway houses, correctional and forensic facilities, crisis centers, detention and rehabilitation centers, disaster relief centers, domestic violence and homeless shelters, drug and alcohol programs, early intervention programs, education at all levels, general hospitals, government agencies, home health agencies, hospices, neonatal nurseries, outpatient clinics, private practice, programs for at-risk youth, programs for persons with disabilities, psychiatric units and hospitals, rehabilitative facilities, senior centers, and wellness centers. Additionally, medical programs for chronic pain, cancer, Alzheimer's, and HIV/AIDS as well as school violence prevention and suicide prevention programs are hiring counselors specializing in the expressive arts (see http://www.nccata.org/ for more information).

Specifically, your work will require you to

- assess client functioning levels, strengths, and areas of need in terms of perceptual, sensory, affective, communicative, artistic, musical, physical, cognitive, social, spiritual, or other abilities;

- develop treatment plans that employ both traditional and expressive arts therapies;

- interact with clients to build rapport and provide emotional support;

- design and provide expressive therapy experiences, using various elements, based on your training and your clients' needs and goals;

- guide clients in exploring their responses to and insights about their encounters with these creative processes; and

- document evaluations, treatment plans, case summaries, and progress or other reports related to individual clients or client groups.

SALARY AND JOB OUTLOOK

There are more than 15,000 Creative Arts Therapists practicing in the United States and around the world (this number includes practitioners of art therapy, dance/movement therapy, drama therapy, music therapy, poetry therapy, and psychodrama; http://www.nccata.org/aboutnccata). If you choose to focus your counseling work in one or more of these areas, your salary will depend on a variety of factors, including education and credentials, experience, population served, and the range of expressive arts you can employ in the service of your clients. Unfortunately, the U.S. Bureau of Labor Statistics does not collect data on creative arts or expressive arts counselors specifically. These professions are part of two other categories: "recreational therapists" and "therapists, all other." Both data sets are presented here.

The median annual wage for recreational therapists was $46,410 in May 2016, with the highest 10 percent earning more than $72,340. In May 2016, the median annual wages for recreational therapists in the top industries in which they worked were as follows (Bureau of Labor Statistics [BLS], 2017a):

- Government $56,670
- Hospitals: state, local, and private $49,030
- Ambulatory healthcare services $47, 320
- Nursing care facilities (skilled) $39,300
- Social assistance $38,490

Most work full time, although about 1 in 5 worked part time in 2016. Some work evenings and weekends to meet the needs of their patients.

In the "therapists, all other" category, the median wage is $56,700 with salaries topping at $95,530 (BLS, 2017b). The average salaries in the industries with the highest levels of employment are

- Office of other health practitioners $53,460
- General medical and surgical hospitals $67,170
- Outpatient care centers $51,960
- Elementary and secondary schools $76,250
- Individual and family services $54,080

BEST PREPARATION

You might consider volunteering in a setting served by counselors who utilize the expressive arts in their practices to observe and better understand the work and determine if it is a good fit for you.

Generally, the practice of expressive therapies requires an educational background in psychology, psychological and behavioral disorders, human development, counseling, therapeutic techniques, and a specific expressive art (art, music, drama, poetry, etc.).

To widen career choices and increase your job prospects in these competitive fields, earning a master's degree in psychology or counseling with an emphasis in one or more of the expressive arts (a master's in the expressive arts is also a degree option) is typically necessary.

SPECIAL CONSIDERATIONS

In most cases, you will maintain professional credentials within your particular expressive arts discipline(s) and also hold state and/or national credentials as counselor.

The following is a list of certifications offered by the various realms of the expressive arts:

- Registered Art Therapist (ATR) or Board Certified Art Therapist (ATR-BC) credentials must be issued by the Art Therapy Credentials Board (http://www.atcb.org/)

- Registered Drama Therapist (RDT) credential is overseen by the North American Drama Therapy Association (http://www.nadta.org/)

- The National Music Therapy Registry (NMTR) serves qualified music therapy professionals with the following designations: RMT, CMT, ACMT.

- Board Certified Music Therapist (MT-BC) credential is issued by the Certification Board for Music Therapists (http://www.cbmt.org/)

- Registered Play Therapist (RPT), Registered Play Therapist-Supervisor (RPT-S), and School Based-Registered Play Therapist (SB-RPT) are credentials offered by the Association for Play Therapy to licensed mental health professionals and school counselors/psychologists

- Certified Poetry Therapist (CPT), Registered Poetry Therapist (PTR), and Certified Applied Poetry Facilitator (CAPF) are credentials offered by International Federation for Biblio/Poetry Therapy (IFB/PT) (http://www.itbpt.com)

ADDITIONAL RESOURCES

American Counseling Association (ACA)	https://www.counseling.org/
American Art Therapy Association (AATA)	www.arttherapy.org
American Dance Therapy Association (ADTA)	www.adta.org/
American Music Therapy Association (AMTA)	www.musictherapy.org
American Society for Group Psychotherapy and Psychodrama	http://www.asgpp.org/index.php
Association for Play Therapy (APT)	http://www.a4pt.org/
The Drama Therapy Fund	http://www.dramatherapyfund.org
International Expressive Arts Therapy Association (IEATA)	http://www.ieata.org/
National Association for Poetry Therapy (NAPT)	http://poetrytherapy.org/
National Coalition of Creative Arts Therapies Associations (NCCATA)	http://www.nccata.org/

MEET THE EXPERTS

Because there are a number of expressive arts that counselors employ in their work with clients, four licensed counselors have provided their thoughts on their careers and offer their views on a counseling practice in the expressive arts: Jennifer Buckler, art therapist; Louise Dimiceli-Mitran, music therapist; Azizi Marshall, drama therapist and expressive arts therapist; and Rachel Wagner-Cantine, dance/movement therapist.

Meet Art Therapist Jennifer Buckler, LCPC, ATR, NCC

What has your career trajectory been? What prompted your decision to become a counselor utilizing the expressive arts?

My career trajectory has led to me work with various populations and professional settings using art therapy counseling. I have worked with residents with dementia in an assisted-living setting; a day treatment alternative school for students with behavioral and emotional difficulties; a social and recreational day program for adults with developmental disabilities; an arts program for adults with developmental disabilities; a behavioral health hospital for children, adolescents, and adults with varying diagnoses and crisis needs; a transition residential school for young adults with physical disabilities; and a group private practice setting for all ages with varying needs. My experiences with providing art therapy counseling within all of these different settings and populations has helped me develop counseling skills that can apply to almost any age, ability, and need. I decided to become a counselor that utilizes expressive arts because I believed at a young age that the arts can help individuals therapeutically as it did for me. Once I learned that there were career opportunities and graduate school programs that support expressive arts therapies, I knew that this was a field that I wanted to pursue.

What is your current job and professional title? How long have you been doing this type of work?

I work as an art therapist at the Center for Creative Arts Therapy, providing art therapy counseling for children, adolescents, and adults with needs that can include anxiety, depression, grief/loss, identity issues, self-esteem issues, and so on within a group private practice setting. I also currently work as an activity therapist at a rehabilitation and education facility providing physical, mental, and expressive therapeutic interventions for young adult students with physical disabilities in a residential transition school setting. I have been practicing art therapy counseling for the past seven years.

Please describe the environment(s) you work in. What are some of the pros and cons of the environment(s)?

I really enjoy my work at the group private practice, Center for Creative Arts Therapy. The work environment is made for the expressive arts therapies and provides ample studio space and art supplies that are conducive for art therapy counseling. The studio space is welcoming and I believe helps supports clients' sense of safety and offers a variety of art supplies for expression needed to explore their feelings and thoughts through art-making. I feel respected at this work environment as an expressive arts therapist professional, and the clients who come in appear to also respect and are interested in expressive arts therapy treatment. The Center for Creative Arts Therapy also employs various expressive arts therapy professional modalities such as dance/movement, art, drama, and music therapy, where clients are able to choose which therapeutic expression is more fitting for their treatment.

My position at the rehabilitation and education facility has been an interesting experience as I've had to provide some inservice information to colleagues so that they can better understand the work that I do with the students using expressive arts therapy. Expressive arts therapy is a relatively new field compared to other counseling approaches, and so sometimes colleagues can be confused on what art therapy or activity therapy is and how it's helping clients. As I have continued my work there, other colleagues and students have provided me with positive feedback and appear to see the progress made through expressive arts therapy.

Please describe a typical day/week at your job.

At the Center for Creative Arts Therapy, my typical day involves seeing individual clients for 1-hour sessions and can include various art therapy interventions depending on the needs, developmental age, and abilities of each client. I am also responsible for writing treatment plans and documenting sessions with progress notes. At the rehabilitation and education facility, my typical day includes art therapy counseling groups; planning and taking students out into the community for recreational opportunities and activities; supervising other volunteers that lead activities for students such as pet therapy, theater instruction, poetry workshops, and others; teaching a leisure education course; teaching a Photoshop course to help students express themselves through technology; and attending IEP [individualized education program] and case management meetings to access students' progress and goals.

What are the best and worst parts of your job and profession?

The best parts of my profession are the opportunity to be creative in designing art therapy interventions and planning recreational activities and opportunities that can help others. I enjoy supporting others and helping them reach their goals. The worst parts of my profession include remembering to take the time for self-care. It's so important to make sure that clinicians keep up with self-care so that they are able to support others to the best of their abilities in treatment.

I have been able to improve my schedule by incorporating more opportunities for self-care, and it has been helping me immensely to do the best I can with supporting clients in treatment.

What would have been helpful to know when you first embarked upon this career?

I think what would have been helpful to know is that finding work in the expressive arts therapy field can be challenging at times. However, I have found that with patience and diligence in searching for employment, it is very possible to find career opportunities and work settings that support the expressive arts therapies.

What should individuals exploring this career consider in order to make the best decision?

When looking for employment as an expressive arts therapist, there are a lot of different populations and settings you can work with, and you should be particular in choosing the right setting and population that you believe fits your skillset.

What is the best preparation for individuals considering this field?

The best preparation is to research the credentialing qualifications of the graduate school programs and post-graduate licensing and certification requirements in your state. It can be confusing, but you'll be most prepared by researching ahead of time and making sure that you follow all the steps necessary in becoming credentialed and licensed in your state. Your licensing and certifications are a necessary part of practicing expressive arts therapy ethically and will support you in finding employment. There are also a lot of different expressive therapy graduate programs out there with different areas of focus and so you want to do your research and choose a graduate program carefully that you believe will fit you best. Also, if you find that colleagues are confused about your work as an expressive therapist in your future employment setting it can be beneficial to provide in-service presentations and offer information about the expressive arts therapy field.

Final thoughts . . . anything else that would be important to know about this work? I

It can be a challenging career field, but overall it's been such a rewarding opportunity for me. I am very happy with this career choice and am excited about my future in this field.

(J. Buckler, personal communication, October 16, 2017)

Meet Music Therapist Louise
Dimiceli-Mitran, MA, LCPC, MT-BC, FAMI

What has your career trajectory been? What prompted your decision to become counselor utilizing the expressive arts?

Unconventional! I received a BME (Bachelor of Music Education) from Drake University and came back to Chicago to the Old Town School of Music to study guitar. After a year, I joined the faculty and taught guitar as my main job for three years. I went on the road for six years after that as a singer/songwriter. After recording an album, I returned to Chicago to work with bands, met and married my musician husband, and had a daughter.

I told a psychologist friend that I might want to become a social worker, and she told me about this field called music therapy. I enrolled in Alverno College—unaware that I could have gone for an MA since I had an undergrad degree in music—for a music therapy equivalency degree and began my first job running dual-diagnosis groups at Gateway Foundation four years later. Here the transformational power of music was so evident as I facilitated stress reduction with music, led instrumental improvisation with percussion instruments to represent their disease, their abusers and supporters; and used guided imagery and music exercises with mandala work, lyric analysis, and songwriting exercises. I loved it! The clients really responded to the nonverbal aspects of treatment that music could offer. I then moved to Advocate Illinois Masonic Hospital to work in outpatient cancer care while pursuing a fellowship in the Bonny Method of Guided Imagery and Music (GIM), which took five years.

I started a private practice in music therapy and GIM and took a part-time music therapy position in oncology at the hospital where I had done my music therapy internship. For 10 years I ran outpatient survivor groups and worked inpatient oncology while using music in many areas in the hospital, including hospice. During that time I got my MA in counseling from Northeastern Illinois University and was able to do my internship at the hospital. I also created the first Midwest training center for GIM out of Indianapolis with my brilliant trainer and colleague, Fran Goldberg. I became a certified GIM trainer through the Association for Music and Imagery and continue to train other professionals in GIM with Fran's Therapeutic Arts Institute. When Fran retires, I will take over Therapeutic Arts and continue the work.

In 2015 I went into full-time private practice where I am today. My life is mostly in my office and teaching GIM. A few years ago I stepped up my songwriting again, started doing a few house concerts, and am now recording an album of new songs. I perform with my daughter singing back-up vocals and my husband on djembe and percussion.

What is your current job and professional title? How long have you been doing this type of work?

Title: Counselor, music psychotherapist and a primary trainer in the Bonny Method of Guided Imagery and Music. I work in my private practice, Rhythms Within LLC, Counseling and Music Psychotherapy, and train other professionals in GIM through the Therapeutic Arts Institute. I started a small music therapy practice in 1997; it continued through my hospital jobs and morphed into a counseling/music psychotherapy practice as it grew. I have added EMDR, mindfulness, and trauma skills to my toolbox.

Please describe the environment(s) you work in. What are some of the pros and cons of the environment(s)? Please describe a typical day/week at your job.

I am grateful for the work environment I have created in my office, furnished with antiques from mothers and grandmothers—it's very comfortable and welcoming.

Pros: Beauty and aesthetics, comfort, easy commute, and some nice professional colleagues in the building. I'm a great boss to myself; my hours are my own. I start at 10 a.m. and have a busy *rush-hour* practice between 4 and 7:30 p.m. I book 30 minutes between clients and have a variety of session times (60 minutes, 90 minutes, and 2 hours), an eclectic clientele, and creativity in my practice. I do verbal therapy, guided imagery, and music experiences (this is a transpersonal therapy and adaptable to many formats), and incorporate EMDR, mandala work, mindfulness, guided imagery without music, and instrumental improvisation into my work with clients. As a client-centered therapist, I'm delighted with the variety and creativity that is part of what I do every day and my clients amaze themselves often.

Cons: I do more administrative work for my practice than I had imagined, filing BCBS insurance.

I'm honestly not sure if the fact that private practice is intense should go under pros or cons! I like intensity most of the time . . .

What are the best and worst parts of your job and profession? What would have been helpful to know when you first embarked upon this career?

Best parts of the job: Creativity and being my own boss! I love seeing the quality of life of my clients improve!

Worst: Marketing. I'm not as comfortable with this as I would like to be. But I invested in a Business School Bootcamp for Therapists class and it really helped me write about what I do, and that was invaluable! I was able to revamp my website and my *Psychology Today* listing. I also receive referrals from other professionals and from clients.

It's been hard because so many people don't know what a music therapist is or the many fields MT-BCs work in. Since becoming a LCPC, I feel more clearly identified but love that I am still practicing my form of music therapy. I'm an outlier in the field, though, having a private practice in mental health and specializing in GIM. Because of my years in the hospital, I have a comfort and knowledge of the effects of physical illness and this is a side specialty of mine. However unusual, the combination of music and verbal work is a great and powerful toolbox in my practice!

I knew almost nothing about music therapy or counseling when I entered school; I have learned about the importance of self-care and running a business along the way! So I'm not sure what I could say about what I wish I knew! The unfolding and lessons learned have been timely and growth inducing.

What should individuals exploring this career consider in order to make the best decision? What is the best preparation for individuals considering this field?

To be a therapist of any kind, you have to have boatloads of compassion, be able to open your nerve endings to be present with people, and think on your feet. Thinking on my feet came with six years of performing onstage in different venues all over the country! I also believe that therapists need to experience their own therapy. It blows me away that some people can go through school without understanding what it is to be in the client's chair. We also have to be able to listen and listen and listen—this is tough all day, especially if some big transition is happening in your private life. Self-care is so important! I meditate and often 20 of those 30 minutes I take between clients is taken up with my chosen form of meditation.

Preparation? Learn to tolerate hard stories, stay grounded no matter what, connect with some type of daily/spiritual practice, and practice patience. If you're a creative arts therapist, prepare by learning about your own creative process and do it! Write, compose, dance, make art—do it all the time. I play guitar and sing most every day because it feeds me; I keep writing music because it feels so good.

Final thoughts . . . anything else that would be important to know about this work?

Creative work with music and other means comes from deep within. Helping clients touch into this space in treatment helps them access their wholeness and the well parts of themselves. This is the quicker and—in my opinion—most effective route through grief, life transitions, trauma, depression, and anxiety and into resilience. The solutions come from within, and those are answers that stick!

(L. Dimiceli-Mitran, personal communication, September 30, 2017)

Meet Drama Therapist and Expressive Arts Therapist Azizi Marshall, MA, LCPC, RDT/BCT, REAT

What has your career trajectory been? What prompted your decision to become a counselor utilizing the expressive arts?

I first started working as a community activist and social justice liaison in St. Louis and Chicago, working with gang violence prevention and incarcerated youth through the use of theater and psychodrama techniques. I then worked as a drama therapist in a residential treatment campus, a therapeutic day school, a cancer wellness center, and multiple private and public high schools. I then ran the Expressive Arts Therapy department at an inpatient psychiatric hospital for five years prior to opening my private practice.

I have served on multiple boards for the North American Drama Therapy Association, as well as several committees and critical incident stress review teams. I am a paid consultant for several law firms and doctoral practices that specialize in at-risk youth and social justice. I am also a speaker, author, and trainer on drama therapy, social justice, community advocacy, and therapeutic performance.

I was raised by two psychodrama-trained, psychotherapist parents who taught me how to stand up for myself and others through their work as activists for battered women and at-risk youth. I knew that theater had an innate ability to heal, educate, and empower others from a young age, and I wanted to make sure others were able to experience these attributes.

What is your current job and professional title? How long have you been doing this type of work?

I am the founder and CEO of the Center for Creative Arts Therapy, an arts-based psychotherapy and training center. We offer the community counseling services by certified creative arts therapists and licensed clinical professionals; additionally, we train clinicians and artists to be certified as a Registered Drama Therapist and Registered Expressive Arts Therapist. I have been doing this type of work for seven years, though I have been a drama therapist for far longer than that.

Please describe the environment(s) you work in. What are some of the pros and cons of the environment(s)?

The Center for Creative Arts Therapy is currently housed in a serene loft building in the suburbs of Chicago. We have a large training/movement/performance room, two art therapy studios, several private offices, two waiting rooms, a few family therapy rooms, a kitchen, and a fabulous team of devoted creative arts therapists.

We are the only center in the country that offers all of the creative arts therapies to the community, internships, and training under one roof. It makes for a very exciting environment! As creative arts therapists we are able to support one another through clinical case supervision, in-house trainings, community support, and the reliance of a billing specialist and marketing coordinator to help make sure things run smoothly.

The challenge that I face as the "boss" is that I am only one person. Sometimes we have to say no to certain community requests. I have learned that saying "no" to something also means we are saying "yes" to something else.

Please describe a typical day/week at your job.

I am typically in the office (Monday–Thursday) by 7:30 a.m. to answer e-mails, return phone calls, pay bills, and so on. I then support my team in planning for marketing initiatives, data entry, billing, and community project preparations.

Around 3 p.m. I start to see clients, and I am typically home around 7:30 p.m. to put my little ones to bed. Throughout the week I attend community meetings to explore potential partnerships to support our community's mental health needs through the arts. Friday night, when my mind is most creative, is sacred. I spend time generating ideas for future projects and updating promotional materials.

What are the best and worst parts of your job and profession?

The best part of my job is seeing a client or student progress through their challenges. It is rewarding to know that I was able to guide that individual or that community to a place of growth and empowerment. I also love staying connected with our students as they navigate their profession as either a drama therapist or expressive arts therapist. I have also enjoyed designing most of our marketing materials and physical space.

The biggest challenge of my profession is the reoccurring conversation I have with people about creative arts therapy. It tends to go a little something like this: "So what do you do?" "Oh, I'm a drama therapist." . . . "Hmm, what's that?"

However, once people have been able to witness or experience drama therapy, they are able to understand the innate healing ability it can have on an individual, family, or community.

What would have been helpful to know when you first embarked upon this career?

How to run a business. It's been a huge crash course for me, and I have had to take additional classes, webinars, and mentorships to grow as a business owner.

Also, you can apply to job openings that may not have "drama therapist" in the title, but one that uses the creative arts. For instance, my first few jobs after becoming registered as a drama therapist were as a therapeutic recreation specialist. Starting out, many of us create jobs as independent contractors.

What should individuals exploring this career consider in order to make the best decision?

You must be skilled as both an artist and as a clinician. You cannot be good at just one, as it takes both the creative side of you *and* the psychologically trained side of you to do the work necessary to guide and heal others.

What is the best preparation for individuals considering this field?

Your internship is when you truly get to experience what it means to be a creative arts therapist. Study your craft and push yourself to learn more about how your craft affects others psychologically. You cannot just create as a creative arts therapist, you must create with a purpose.

Final thoughts . . . anything else that would be important to know about this work?

You will find great passion in the work. Never forget why you chose this path, and how you are uniquely positioned to create change.

(A. Marshall, personal communication, October 8, 2017)

Meet Dance/Movement Therapist Rachel Wagner-Cantine, LCPC, BC-DMT

What has your career trajectory been? What prompted your decision to become a counselor utilizing the expressive arts?

Residential treatment with Department of Children and Family Services wards as a DMT; foster care and adoption/community-based care as clinical therapist; for-profit residential treatment with women (mood, ED, SA, trauma) and as a DMT/mood and trauma specialist/group therapist, and private practice.

Dance was an integral part of my life through childhood into college. It was a therapeutic outlet for me. I always knew dance would be some part of my career. Finding DMT was a perfect union of my interest in psychology and dance.

What is your current job and professional title? How long have you been doing this type of work?

I am a Licensed Counselor and Dance/Movement Therapist and own a private practice. I also am a contract therapist with the Center for Creative Arts Therapy. I've been doing this type of work for 10 years in various settings and have been in this "job/role" for three years.

Please describe the environment(s) you work in. What are some of the pros and cons of the environment(s)?

Private practice owner and contract therapist. I have my own clients that I schedule and bill, and pay for usage of space and all other expenses. I'm also contracted with the center where they provide clients, billing, space and materials, and marketing, and we have a split of profits.

My own practice, pros: Independence, full retention of profits, freedom of population choice. Cons: Lonely, more expenses, requires more operation/business tasks, must deal with insurance directly, everything falls on me.

Contract therapist, pros: Support and camaraderie, little to no operation/business tasks. Cons: Less retention of direct service profit.

Please describe a typical day/week at your job.

I see clients Sunday through Wednesday. Some days are full + days (11 a.m. – 8 or 9 p.m.) and include paperwork (progress notes), billing, session prep, and usually 3–6 sessions. Other days I just come in for sessions.

What are the best and worst parts of your job and profession?

Best: Helping others, working with other creative people, being able to connect with the arts and guide clients in doing so, providing a safe and secure relationship to clients (especially with trauma), and freedom to be myself and be creative.

Worst: Dealing with insurance companies and the inconsistent pay, not always having control (e.g., clients can terminate at any time), the business side (marketing, promotion, etc.).

What would have been helpful to know when you first embarked upon this career?

Knowing that I should really push my own therapy/supervision and keep it consistent outside of workplace supervision has been very important. It would have been really useful to know that I don't have to work with every population—it's okay to be picky. And finally, to know that we will always have to explain what DMT is.

What should individuals exploring this career consider in order to make the best decision?

Are you willing to do your own therapy/self-exploration? The system is difficult and will most likely never change. Money should not be your main focus. You'll never stop being challenged and learning more about yourself and the work.

What is the best preparation for individuals considering this field?

In-field observation/shadowing—push to reflect on why you are drawn to this field.

Final thoughts . . . anything else that would be important to know about this work?

It's incredibly challenging (and that never stops), and worth it.

(R. Wagner-Cantine, personal communication, October 6, 2017)

References

Bureau of Labor Statistics (BLS), U.S. Department of Labor. (2017a). Recreational therapists. *Occupational outlook handbook.* Retrieved from https://www.bls.gov/ooh/healthcare/recreational-therapists.htm

Bureau of Labor Statistics), U.S. Department of Labor (BLS). (2017b). *Occupational employment and wages, May 2016: 29-1129 Therapists, all other.* Retrieved from https://www.bls.gov/oes/current/oes291129.htm

Malchiodi, C. (2014, June 30). Creative arts therapy and expressive arts therapy. *Psychology Today.* Retrieved from https://www.psychologytoday.com/blog/arts-and-health/201406/creative-arts-therapy-and-expressive-arts-therapy

Pehrsson, D.-E. (2009). Creative arts in counseling. *The ACA encyclopedia of counseling* (pp. 130–131). Alexandria, VA: American Counseling Association.

8

MARRIAGE, COUPLES, AND FAMILY COUNSELORS

A DAY IN THE LIFE

"Because the self is deeply embedded in relationships, a client's dilemmas are frequently healed through relationships. This also implied that change in the client's life affects others with whom the client comes in contact. Moreover, failure to consider how others may be affected by client change may undermine the change process and runs the risk of posing damage to intimate relationships." (Falke, 2009, p. 196)

As a marriage, couples, and family counselor, you will work with individuals, couples, and families, providing treatment through a family-centered lens. You will not only be treating your clients but also their relationships. Your goals will be to help individuals, couples, or families manage or overcome problems of daily living as well as mental and emotional disorders, and do so in the context of their families and relationships. You will listen and ask questions about family roles and development to help clients understand their problems and develop strategies to improve their lives. Marriage, couples, and family counselors must be effective in working with a variety of issues including low self-esteem; poor communication; stress; addiction and substance abuse; illness; grief and loss; separation and divorce; physical, emotional, or sexual abuse; depression; anxiety; and more severe psychopathology.

Specifically, as a marriage, couples, and family counselor, you will

- collect information about clients, using techniques such as testing, interviewing, discussion, and observation;

- develop treatment plans using a family systems lens to address family relationship problems, destructive patterns of behavior, and other personal issues;

- counsel clients regarding personal and interpersonal issues (i.e., parenting, financial concerns, work/life balance);

- teach skills and strategies to clients and their families to help them communicate constructively and manage and/or resolve problems effectively;

- encourage clients to discuss their emotions, behaviors, and experiences;

- help clients process their reactions and adjust to difficult transitions in their lives, such as separation, divorce, job loss;

- assist clients in developing strategies and skills to change their behavior and improve their ability to cope with challenging circumstances;

- guide clients through the process of making and acting upon decisions about their future;

- refer clients to other resources or services in the community, such as support groups or inpatient treatment facilities; and

- maintain case files that include activities, progress notes, evaluations, and recommendations.

SALARY AND JOB OUTLOOK

The median salary for marriage and family counselors is approximately $49,170, with the highest earners making about $82,000 annually. There are 41,500 marriage and family therapists currently employed in the United States. The growth rate for this career is 20 percent through 2026, which is considerably higher than average (Bureau of Labor Statistics [BLS], 2017).

In May 2016, the median annual wages for marriage and family counselors in the top industries in which they worked were as follows (BLS, 2017):

- State and local government, excluding education and hospitals $72,180

- Outpatient care centers $48,900

- Offices of other health practitioners $47,650

- Individual and family services $44,560

Other organizations that employ marriage and family counselors are general and private hospitals, community mental health centers, substance abuse treatment facilities, employee assistance programs, and private practice.

BEST PREPARATION

All states require marriage and family therapists to have a master's degree in counseling or marriage and family therapy and a license to practice. It may also be useful to check the Commission on Accreditation for Marriage and Family Therapy Education website (http://www.coamfte.org/) when considering focusing your master's degree in marriage and family counseling or seeking a post-master's certification.

SPECIAL CONSIDERATION

For information about MFT licensure exam, go to Association of Marital & Family Regulatory Boards at https://amftrb.org/

ADDITIONAL RESOURCES

American Association of Marriage and Family Therapy	http://www.aamft.org/
American Counseling Association	http://www.counseling.org
American Family Therapy Academy	https://afta.org/
International Association of Marriage and Family Counselors	http://www.aamft.org
International Family Therapy Association	http://www.ifta-familytherapy.org/
National Council on Family Relations	https://www.ncfr.org/

MEET ANTONIO ROMANO, LCPC, SFBT

What has your career trajectory been? What prompted your decision to become a marriage and family counselor?

I have a law degree from another country, and my initial thought was to obtain a degree in the United States as well in order to practice international law. Obviously it did not work out that way. I have always been interested in psychology and human behavior, and I tried to focus on those aspects—even in law school—by electing to take classes on forensic psychology and abnormal behavior. When I moved to the United States, although I was proud to have been accepted into law school, I quickly discovered that a legal career was not for me, given the many panic attacks I was experiencing while in pre-law classes.

I then began my own self-work with a Jungian analyst. It kept me quite busy for years until I realized that the ability to help and provide alleviation to human suffering was something that felt natural to me. At that point, I began to pursue a career in counseling.

What is your current job and professional title? How long have you been doing this type of work?

I am an LCPC and currently work in an outpatient hospital setting. I have been working as a counselor for over 10 years.

Please describe the environment you work in. What are some of the pros and cons of the environment?

My environment is an atypical mental health center as it is also an intense training campus for doctoral residents who usually spend a year or two completing their fellowship or post-doc. The pros of this type of environment are many: an eclectic population of patients, ongoing supervision, and the possibility to take a didactic stance with the student/residents, as most licensed therapists become mentors in helping residents better define their clinical character for their future role as therapists. It is a great opportunity for students who are thrown into the midst of this type of work and need to think on their feet to successfully navigate this challenging clinical environment. It is also a great opportunity for supervisors to review and check their clinical stance. Additionally, the environment encourages supervisors to pursue professional development to more effectively counsel clients directly or indirectly through supervisory discussion. Another advantage of this type of setting is the diverse population it serves, which calls for increasing clinical as well as technical knowledge. It does require particular skills to recognize the limitations of clinical interventions in the face of resistant clients or mental illness chronicity that can only be improved so much.

The cons are more related to the extensive hours required. A multitude of daily tasks can sharpen our abilities to multitask; on the other hand, it reduces time for consultation, self-development and self-preparation—and I believe that it is the client who pays the price in the end. We understand the difficulties of accommodating an eclectic number of insurers who call for different types of treatment in terms of duration, typology of intervention, and resources; however, large hospitals have acquiesced to the science of "survival," which requires the clinic to adapt to what may be essential for its existence. My clinic is not an exception to this rule.

Please describe a typical day/week at your job.

A typical day at my job begins with checking phone calls and messages. Messages will determine the level of stress of my day, alongside the caseload of clients I have to see. Clients may vary and they usually come as referrals from the ER next to us or by other doctors operating within the same network as our clinic. On a typical day, I also have responsibilities as a supervisor since our campus is a training ground for externs and residents pursuing a career in counseling or in psychology.

What is typical, therefore, is to expect the unexpected; your plans of leaving on time are ideal wishes that rarely come true. Paperwork in a hospital setting is intense; there is a great deal of time dedicated to the completion of documents. Seeing clients after all seems to be the "easier" part, or the part we studied so passionately for. Even though you may face challenging cases most of the time, on that "typical day" there is always the hope that we have helped that particular client, couple, or family see the world as a place to rejoin in spite of the fears, the sadness, and the difficulties in doing so. There is an inner awareness that this is what we have chosen above all: above fame, above financial stability, social approval, or disapproval. We have chosen to stick to the vagaries of our effectiveness/ineffectiveness, often not knowing what has changed in the chemistry of the clients' relationship with their pain. We have chosen to be okay with the absence of our clients' spoken recognition that we have helped them to see themselves as a decent, dignified, worthy human beings. This is what we essentially have bargained for when we have chosen to be counselors.

What are the best and worst parts of your job/profession?

I think that helping others in need must come from a deeper place. We all help others regardless of what we do. One way or another we perform some kind of activity that helps others. The difference in the counseling arena is the quality of such help that requires not only skills but a deeper sense of humility in wanting to accept the pain of others as the main theme of our life. I am not sure that I can talk about counseling others in terms of what is best or worst, although I can honestly say that positive and negative moments are parts of the same continuum and, at the end of the day, they are both essential to develop our awareness of what clients need. Obviously no one wants to be wrong, but it is extremely hard to judge the nature of this job in terms of right or wrong. The best possible way to understand what is important is to remain open to options and realize that there are many solutions to one problem, whether we are right about it or not. What is right, if we could use such an expression, is the human dilemma, the existential quest for a better life our clients claim and bring forth within themselves in front of us.

What would have been helpful to know when you first embarked upon this career?

Definitely knowing the nature of this commitment and the quality of it is something that comes to mind. On the other hand, I am not sure about predictability factors. This is a job that has lots of mysteries, and not knowing how to exactly deal with it is one of those mysteries. I am not talking about technical or clinical preparation; that is there and everyone to a different degree achieves a certain level of proficiency. I am referring to the life changes that the profession entails—such as not knowing who we will be and how we will change in the course of our journey with our clients. This aspect of the profession would have been helpful to know but it also would have been a different career, had that been the case.

What should individuals exploring this career consider in order to make the best decision?

People should consider whether true listening is their true vocation. Listening is not about selecting what's important or being positive or negative: it is about not assuming; it is about taking a neutral stance in order to facilitate whatever clients are processing about themselves, each other, and the world. We are all tempted to give clues to others about the map of emotions and associated actions. We need to stay firm on not having convictions, personal values, and life suggestions. Not because we do not have them but because it would be too easy to feel effective just by matching the client's world with suggestions and opinions. We mostly match the client's feelings and desires—after all, that is how we account for their vulnerability. We can only offer a place for individuals, partners, and families that may help them clarify what they want and how they define themselves. Staying out of their path is the goal, although our presence is essential for them to recognize that there is a path that is worthwhile to explore.

What is the best preparation for individuals considering this field?

From a structural standpoint school is necessary: classes provide a wealth of information that students must have. However, schoolwork must be accompanied by a strong opportunity for students to experience what they learn in the classroom. Confidence cannot be tested in the classroom. The ability to sit before a client and accept silence as a sign of treatment resistance needs to be experienced on the novice's skin and such experience needs to be processed through appropriate supervision. A class can teach students how to make a differential diagnosis or whether a specific diagnosis fits the cluster of symptoms presented by the client. However, it cannot replace the hands-on perception of the student about the client's experience.

The discovery of whether someone can be a mental health professional starts when tools, technical words, and clinical definitions have run their course and there are not more books to read; and that happens quite quickly. *Being with the client* is different than *diagnosing the client*; a formative internship will focus on the former aspect of the client/therapist's relationship, thus helping the novice therapist understand that at times technical knowledge could result in a form of avoidance when the therapist utilizes labeling as a way of not dealing with the real issue.

In most cases, the issue is the discomfort or despair that has led our clients to seek help. If we are stuck in the desert without water and we come to a pond (the only one in miles), we would hope to be able to drink from it without having to invest too much time in figuring out how to do it when our life is at risk. Therapy starts with the ability to be this "pond" for our clients so that they can have immediate access to it, once everything else has failed them. But such ability to mirror clients' needs requires compassion and true concern as much as neutrality and objectivity. This balance is one of the most difficult to reach as our clients may engender all kinds of emotions in us, often leaving inexperienced therapists at the mercy of their own feelings, doubts, and fears of not being helpful. Therefore, even though academic preparation is essential, a formative internship that includes appropriate and competent supervision all around is also indispensable. The lack of such experience may in fact create an irreparable divide between professional knowledge and professional behavior.

Final thoughts . . . anything else that would be important to know about this work?

Another aspect to consider in counseling, which is at times discounted, is the importance of couples and family therapy. We are usually so focused on the client that we fail to realize that their suffering is always the product of other variables separated from the specific disorder and yet intrinsically connected to it. When a client comes in with symptoms of depression or anxiety we usually target the acuity of these symptoms and provide interventions to alleviate them. At times, we do not recognize that part of the client's discomfort comes from within the self and is the result of the client's relationship with the world.

Symptoms or emotional dysregulation do not exist as a biological inner event; they are usually connected with people in the client's life, starting with families and ending with friends. When we deal with emotionally dysregulated clients we have to ask ourselves how they got to be so. This question, more than diagnostic, is systemic, referring to the level of understanding and validation the individual has been receiving from his or her surroundings, primarily caregivers, family members, and friends. If the struggles associated with depression or anxiety are just seen as an individual problem the client cannot solve, we would have missed the target of treatment.

The world of the client is not disassociated from their relationships; and, how much support, understanding, and overall validation the client receives from them will dictate his or her level of success in managing and eventually overcoming struggles. The struggles are not about the symptoms; rather, the symptoms signal that the client does not match the environment in a way that is functional and makes sense to him or her. But what needs to match is also how the environment understands the client. Therefore, partners and/or family members are an essential part of the client's recovery as their validation of the client's condition will serve the purpose of normalizing the client and reprogramming what the client needs to function within his or her immediate world and eventually with the world at large.

The lack of understanding of some therapists that the problem stems from the client in conjunction with his or her environment can deepen the client's problem and constitute a real barrier to healing. Therefore, the approach for the most part is systemic and not individually driven. When we work with individual clients, especially adolescents, we must consider the level of acceptance of the client's environment that often refuses to take any responsibility for the client's malfunctioning. When colleagues ask me if I can take a case involving family or couple's therapy because they do not feel comfortable with it, I always think of them as surgeons who decide to operate without the help of the anesthesiologist in their team. No competent surgeon would do that and nor should a competent therapist. In a world in which complexities are faced with technology and brief interventions, it is even more important to have full participation in treatment of the people that matter in a client's life. Their contribution, even solely for the purpose of understanding their role in client's situation, may increase the chances of delivering a more adequate and targeted support to client.

For couples work, the same concept is just as valid. We cannot understand why things don't work for a client if we do not assess their ability to effectively communicate and interact with the world, whether their world is boyfriend, girlfriend, husband, wife, partner, or significant other. A way to identify what is not working for the client is by seeing the client in action. For instance, how the client handles pressures in a couple's session may provide useful information about the type of individual work the client may need to do outside of the couple's therapy. A therapist that underplays the importance of a systemic approach may risk increasing the client's suffering instead of opening the door to personal transformation that is best achieved if the environment of family and significant relationships is present in the therapy room.

(A. Romano, personal communication, October 15, 2017)

References

Bureau of Labor Statistics, U.S. Department of Labor. (2017). Marriage and family therapists. *Occupational outlook handbook*. Retrieved from https://www.bls.gov/ooh/community-and-social-service/marriage-and-family-therapists.htm

Falke, S. I. (2009). Family counseling. *The ACA encyclopedia of counseling* (pp. 195–196). Alexandria, VA: American Counseling Association.

ORGANIZATIONAL COUNSELORS

A DAY IN THE LIFE

Choosing to be an organizational counselor typically means you will be spending your time as a part of the human resources function of the organization. Overall, you will be working to expand the knowledge and effectiveness of employees in order to accomplish organizational change and improve individual satisfaction and performance. Your role, depending on the type of employer and the specifics of your job, may include policy planning, employee training and development, leadership development, succession planning, organizational diagnosis and troubleshooting, and strategic planning. You must maintain relationships with line employees and management as you work to both advance the goals of your employer and listen and respond to the concerns and the wisdom of the organization's workers. It will be critical to your effectiveness to keep up with organizational development research and understand the impact of global, cultural, economic, and technological changes. Most often, you will find employment in large for-profit or nonprofit organizations, consultancy, or education.

In summary, as an organizational counselor, you will

- assess employees' needs for training, align the training with the organization's strategic goals, and evaluate its effectiveness;

- teach training methods and skills to instructors and supervisors;

- identify policy issues and work with leadership to create and/or revise policy based on organizational goals and best practices;

- note positive or problem patterns in the organization's culture and bring them to the attention of appropriate stakeholders; and

- review and research organizational and leadership development literature to bring cutting-edge information to discussions with the organization's leadership team, managers, and individual employees.

SALARY AND JOB OUTLOOK

Once again, the area of organizational counseling is not specifically addressed by the Bureau of Labor Statistics, thus the use of the statistics collected for "training and development manager," which is the most closely aligned occupation for which data are collected. The median annual wage was $115,180 in May 2016. The lowest 10 percent earned less than $57,760, and the highest 10 percent earned more than $184,990. This field is projected to grow at a higher than average rate, or about 10 percent through 2026 (Bureau of Labor Statistics [BLS], 2017a).

In May 2016, the median annual wages for this field and the top industries were as follows (BLS, 2017b):

- Management of companies and enterprises $114,290

- Professional, scientific, and technical services $113,310

- Finance and insurance $109,650

- Educational services; state, local, private $99,040

- Healthcare and social assistance $96,910

Work is usually full time during business hours, but your days may be longer than 9 to 5. Depending on your organization, travel may be involved (BLS, 2017a).

If you are interested in this occupation, you may also find it useful to review the BLS info on I/O psychology in regards to salary and job outlook (BLS, 2017c).

BEST PREPARATION

Graduates with a master's degree in organizational counseling or industrial/organizational (I/O) psychology can work as organizational counselors. Education in human resources management, organizational development, business administration, or information technology is also very useful.

Beyond education, work experience—especially in the type of organizations you are interested in working for as an organizational counselor—is a must-have.

SPECIAL CONSIDERATIONS

This occupation offers several certifications:

- Associate Professional in Talent Development (APTD) offered by the Association for Talent Development and focused on talent development professionals who are in the early part of their careers or whose professional roles and aspirations are focused on a few areas of expertise.

- Certified Professional in Learning & Performance (CPLP) offered by the Association for Talent Development.

- Certified Performance Technologist (CPT) offered by the International Society for Performance Improvement.

ADDITIONAL RESOURCES

Association for Talent Development	https://www.td.org/
International Society for Performance Improvement	http://www.ispi.org
Society for Human Resource Management	http://www.shrm.org
Society for Industrial and Organizational Psychology	http://www.siop.org

MEET RICK RITTMASTER, MA

Please describe your career trajectory.

An organizational counselor's career path is certainly more curvy than straight. I've found in my own career that organizational counselors tend to be located in human resources, as is the case with my current role. However, many of the skillsets that an organizational counselor must develop often mirror effective leadership; so if an organizational counselor is interested or willing to develop business acumen then there is almost no limit to the impact they can have in an organization. My personal career trajectory involves finding new and creative ways to use my skills to unlock the passions of others, which (hopefully) will lead to a very broad and diverse set of roles and responsibilities.

What is your job and professional title? How long have you been doing this type of work?

I am the learning and development manager at MTS Systems. I work with individuals at all levels of the organization to ensure that employees are engaged in the work they are doing, as well as building skills that align with the needs (current and future) of my company. I like my job because I get to work on big projects that affect the entire employee population, as well as help individual people improve the skills they use for daily work. From the biggest, broadest perspective I believe my role is to help people find purpose in what they do, and build skills that also translate into stronger communities.

I'd like to think this career path really got started when I was an intern under Cam Helkowski at the Loyola University Chicago Career Development Center. In that sense, I've been at this work just under 10 years.

Please describe the environment(s) you work in. What are some of the pros and cons of the environment(s)?

I think that my environment can be described in two ways: the unique culture of my current organization, MTS Systems, and the environment that is general to the nature of an organizational counselor. I believe that people are people; and, once you figure out how to work with people, then that skill will be mostly transferable wherever you go. So to be successful in this field I believe you must genuinely love working with people. I do, and this is a big pro for my work. I love learning a person's "story" and why they are interested in what they do. I also have a lot of flexibility and creativity in how I approach my work. I might coach individuals who are unsatisfied, or use this person's experience to identify a more systemic challenge that the organization is facing. A drawback to this environment is that sometimes this work can be perceived as limiting rather than promoting an organization's ability to be successful. At an organizational level, not all companies are interested in investing in these services for employees. And at an individual level, not all employees are interested in pursuing the truths that empower and unlock their potential.

I currently work for a highly technical and engineering-focused organization. In essence, I work with a bunch of engineers. As someone whose primary focus is encouraging and promoting "soft skills," I often find myself a fish out of water. Because of the technical nature of my company I've learned to shift how I share ideas, and whenever possible I share data that reflect studies, outcomes, or research that has been done to "validate" the positive impacts of improved leadership, communication, and collaboration.

Please describe a typical day/week at your job.

There is nothing "cookie cutter" about being an organizational counselor, which is both a great gift and, at times, a significant challenge. It's often a balance between meeting individual needs and supporting MTS [organizational] goals and objectives. However, if I was to bucket my regular activities, it would probably look something like this:

Leading projects and process. This is probably where I spend the majority of my time. A big part of my role is ensuring that organization-wide processes, like performance management and leadership development, are running smoothly and making a positive impact. As I mentioned, I lead the Performance Management guidance team. We ensure that the tools, resources, and processes that support performance discussions help managers and employees do their jobs more effectively. These projects and processes help others find deeper meaning in their work.

Consulting and counseling. A significant percentage of my job is spent consulting on effective organizational psychological and organizational development practices. While the content differs, the process facilitating these discussions directly mirrors a traditional counseling conversation. On a daily basis I practice deep listening skills, ask questions to probe toward underlying issues, and provide different perspectives that build internal motivation toward a future state. Honestly, the more I practice as an organizational counselor the more grateful I am that I have a background in the art of counseling.

Learning. I make it a very conscious activity to know my colleagues, both in terms of their daily work and their values and beliefs. I ask many questions to help align my efforts with the goals and objectives that are important to MTS. And I maintain my skillset by reading about new trends, networking with colleagues in this field, and thinking about how to apply new ideas to make MTS better. I'm only as good as my ability to apply my skillsets in a meaningful context to the people I work with. This requires a healthy approach toward the act of learning.

What are the best and worst parts of your job and profession?

The best part of my job is that moment when a crucial insight is unlocked that helps an individual, team, or even the entire company find more meaning in their work. This act of unlocking meaning also can start a process that leads to more engaged employees, more effective companies, and stronger communities. Getting to play a role in this process is a true gift.

The worst part of my job is managing skepticism. Throughout my career I have run into various (and to be fair, often valid) concerns about the focus of my role. Typical skepticism ranges from the outright "you don't represent the real world" to the more restrained "show me the value that you provide my team, department, career, etc." These conversations aren't without value. I'm in a business setting; I want to provide a business case for this work. Also, I need to meet people where they really are, and sometimes managing skepticism is educating about what it is that I do. This is especially true when people "have" to, rather than "get" to, work with an organizational counselor. The fancy term for this concept is managing resistance. I've gotten better at it. But, skepticism will always limit the full impact of my work.

What would have been helpful to know when you first embarked upon this career?

When I first started I was in my late 20s, and I spent a lot of time worrying that I would be perceived as less qualified because of my age and experience. I've learned that the opportunity to help others be better leaders and find meaning in their work is large. Like, really big. As in, this is going to be one of the main issues facing the entire workforce in the coming generation, and successful companies will be the ones who figure out how to tap into a person's sense and desire for purpose. So if you have good training on how to help others in these areas, then trust your training. Lean into every opportunity you get to guide toward the path of a more meaningful career; chances are overwhelmingly likely that they will appreciate your time and investment. Because again, the need is big, and the number of people focused on solving these issues is, by comparison, quite small.

But also, be wary of positioning yourself as having "answers." There is only one quote hanging up at my desk and it reads, "Double your questions to statements ratio." It comes from the author Jim Collins, and as you can probably guess the intent is to drive people toward understanding each other better, not necessarily to advertise expertise. Many talented organizational counselors, and indeed many professionals in general, can be derailed quickly by abandoning this pursuit.

What should individuals exploring this career consider in order to make the best decision?

If you're considering this field then ask yourself these questions: "Can I stay committed to my own values?" and, "Am I comfortable working with people who fail multiple times?"

I've worked with other organizational counselors that haven't been able to answer those questions, and the negative impact is significant. Organizational counselors can become order takers, executing the wishes of other third parties (senior leaders, shareholders, team members, etc.). This is dangerous because an organizational counselor's goal is to help bring out and foster those passions, not to instruct on the best/most valuable passion that the employee "should" have. Likewise, an organizational counselor who is overly academic or dogmatic in their approach is equally dangerous. Instead of helping draw out passion, they squash any attempt at insightful dialogue because correct process is not being followed. I call this the "yoga teacher yelling at yoga students for not practicing enough yoga" effect. No one is perfect; organizational counselors must aim to provide help to those in need, regardless of the context.

As I've mentioned, organizational counselors are in some sense fish out of water. We're asking people to change in ways that often don't directly translate to immediate results. Business (in general) rewards quick fixes and fast progress. Our work is decidedly slower, and to be successful requires both patience and perseverance. One of my favorite sayings about strength is that "it is a strong tree that bends in the wind." Without good roots, the tree blows away. Without adequate flexibility, the tree breaks. So, too, is the work of an organizational counselor.

What is the best preparation for individuals considering this field?

I recommend two main experiences when preparing to enter the field of organizational counseling. The first is to gain general business experience. And when I say general, I mean general; any experience where you have a boss, a set of regular tasks, and a team to work with will do (although preferably experience outside of human resources). This advice is especially important for students coming right out of school. One of the biggest, and most valid, frustrations with organizational counselors is that they do not understand what it is like to be a "line employee." I spent the first year of my working experience as a customer service representative, and it was one of the most valuable experiences of my career.

Second, I would strongly encourage some formal training around the practice of counseling others. It is risky for organizational counselors not to have some training around the process, tools, and skillsets that support helping individuals learn and grow. Without this training an organizational counselor may either misunderstand, or worse, mistreat the needs of an individual. This training also informs when to refer out to the care of other counselors. I graduated with a master's degree in organizational psychology, and I found it did an excellent job preparing me for this work. My education helped me understand how to work with employees and create change at an individual level, but then also how to work with groups of people to create change that positively impacts the systems within an organization. I use my counseling skillsets on a daily basis, and I am very grateful to have a focused understanding of when I can, and can't, offer help.

Final thoughts . . . anything else that would be important to know about this work?

Right now organizational counseling is experiencing a lot of fascinating change. There are a collection of macro-trends coalescing that are having, and will continue to have, a tremendous impact on the way that we work. The rise of the millennial generation, increased pace of globalism, the "gig economy," increased emphasis on socially conscious organizations, virtual teams, and mobile working are some great examples of these changes. Any of these trends will need organizational counselors to help translate them into meaningful work experiences for organizations. Additionally, there is a deluge of new and exciting research that is providing evidence-based practices to help push this field forward and define best practices. There is so much opportunity to be a part of this exciting future.

However, as much as organizational counseling changes, its core remains the same. Organizational counseling is first and foremost about working with people. Trends may shift the application, but the drive to help others find purpose and passion will always remain constant.

(R. Rittmaster, personal communication, September 19, 2017)

References

Bureau of Labor Statistics, U.S. Department of Labor. (2017a). Occupational employment and wages, May 2016: 11-3131 training and development managers. *Occupational employment statistics.* Retrieved from https://www.bls.gov/oes/current/oes113131.htm

Bureau of Labor Statistics, U.S. Department of Labor. (2017b). Training and development managers. *Occupational outlook handbook, 2016–17 edition.* Retrieved from https://www.bls.gov/ooh/management/training-and-development-managers.htm

Bureau of Labor Statistics, U.S. Department of Labor. (2017c). *Occupational employment statistics: Occupational employment and wages, May 2016—19-3032 industrial-organizational psychologists.* Retrieved from https://www.bls.gov/oes/current/oes193032.htm#st

PASTORAL
COUNSELORS

A DAY IN THE LIFE

"Pastoral counselors hold a unique position in the field of counseling. With their combination of theological training and advanced education in the behavioral sciences, they are poised to provide effective mental health counseling that is capable of respectfully integrating religious and spiritual components." (Walker, Scheidegger, End, & Amundsen, 2012, p. 16)

As a pastoral counselor, you will provide clinical mental health services to individuals, couples, families, and groups of all ages and circumstances. What is unique about your treatment process is your ability to integrate religion and spirituality and offer therapy in a faith-based or values-based context should it prove desirable and/or beneficial to your clients. Beyond providing psychotherapy, you might also choose to employ prayer, religious and/or spiritual readings, and other forms of spiritually based exploration to guide your clients in a practice of healing and enhancing body, mind, and spirit.

An increased interest in spiritually integrated counseling and psychotherapy is not surprising given the 2015 Pew Research Center study that found that 89 percent of adults believe in "God or a universal spirit" and in the 2012 study by Pew that determined that 8 in 10 people (worldwide) identify with a religious group (Snodgrass, 2017). While people may engage with you around an array of mental health concerns, your training makes you particularly suited to work with individuals facing grief and loss, chronic illness, end of life concerns, a crisis of faith, mental health issues directly linked to religious beliefs or doctrine, and reintegration into community life after institutionalization or incarceration.

You will have a variety of work environments to choose from including hospitals, hospice centers, colleges and universities, nonprofits, faith communities, counseling centers, inpatient programs, correctional facilities, domestic violence centers, substance abuse programs, long-term care facilities, and private practice. In the course of your work in these situations, you may be offering a range of services in addition to counseling individuals, couples, and families. Group work—clinical, spiritual, and psycho-educational—is often part of the job description of pastoral counselors. Some settings, like hospitals or shelters, may require a more solution-focused style; while others, like colleges, faith communities, or private practice, may offer the option for longer-term therapeutic approaches and spiritual direction. "Today, rigorous research methods are used to demonstrate the effectiveness of pastoral counseling and spiritually-integrated mental health care. Pastoral counselors are urged to ground their counseling theories and practices in evidence-based methods and to contribute to the growing body of research" (Snodgrass, 2017).

Specifically, as a pastoral counselor, you will

- use the dual lenses and techniques of psychotherapy and spirituality to collect information about clients and develop treatment plans;

- counsel individuals, couples, and families on a range of mental health concerns as well as developmental and crisis issues that arise in the course of daily living;

- teach skills and strategies to clients and their families to help them communicate more effectively and support each other through resolution of issues and/or crisis;

- assess clients' interest/need and integrate spiritual and religious components (i.e., prayer, readings, rituals) into clinical practice as appropriate;

- facilitate counseling, psychoeducational, and spiritual direction groups; and

- maintain case files that include activities, progress notes, evaluations, and recommendations.

SALARY AND JOB OUTLOOK

Because salary and job outlook information is not available from the U.S. Bureau of Labor Statistics (BLS) for the profession of pastoral counselor, we will review BLS data for occupations that are the closest match: marriage and family therapists, all mental health counselors, and clergy. Your salary will be determined by your own experience as well as the environments and populations that are the focus of your work.

Projected growth for all mental health counseling is above average at about 20 percent through 2026 (BLS, 2017a), and the field of marriage and family therapy is projected to grow at about the same rate during this period of time (BLS, 2017b). Projected growth for clergy is average (about 8 percent), with 29,200 projected job openings through 2026 (BLS, 2017c). As of May 2016 the average salary for all mental health counselors was $42,840 (BLS, 2017a), and marriage and family therapists averaged $49,170 (BLS, 2017b). The average annual salary for clergy was $45,740 (BLS, 2017c). Please see Chapters 6 and 9 for expanded employment information.

BEST PREPARATION

While educational pathways to a career as a pastoral counselor vary, it is generally accepted that the best preparation is a master's degree program in pastoral counseling. Earning this type of degree secures your eligibility for licensure in your state. Additionally, this distinctive training, given education in theology, spirituality, and religion as well as psychology and the behavioral sciences, will allow you to offer your clients both psychological competence and theological congruence.

SPECIAL CONSIDERATIONS

Certifications

For many years, the American Association of Pastoral Counselors (AAPC) was the certification and licensing body for the profession of pastoral counseling. In light of the role that state and provincial governments now have in regulating licensure, the AAPC has recently discontinued this practice. However, pastoral counselors (who have a master's degree in counseling) are candidates for state licensure and the National Certified Counselor (NCC) certification, as well as other specialty certifications.

Ethical Questions to Consider

There are three areas of ethical concern of which pastoral counselors must be aware (GoodTherapy.org, n.d.):

- Dual Relationships—The AAPC Code of Ethics explains that pastoral counselors are to take every precaution to avoid confusing dual/multiple relationships. This may prove particularly taxing for pastoral counselors who are also ministers in faith communities.

- Confidentiality—The role of confidentiality for clergy can differ from confidentiality requirements of mental health professionals. Pastoral counselors who are also in ministry may encounter dilemmas if the ethical codes of the organizations that govern them do not define confidentiality in the same way.

- Standard of Care—Because not all pastoral counselors are licensed, the standards of care may differ. This can be a possible concern for people receiving counseling from those practicing outside of the umbrella of a professional counseling organization. It may also alter the perception that potential clients have of the efficacy of pastoral counseling.

ADDITIONAL RESOURCES

American Counseling Association   www.counseling.org
American Association of Pastoral Counselors   www.aapc.org/

MEET ALISON TOBACK, MA, MAPC, LCPC

What has your career trajectory been? What prompted your decision to become a pastoral counselor?

Before becoming a pastoral counselor, I had a 17-year career in adult literacy. Although clients suffered from the significant stresses related to low income, they tended to resist the free counseling services offered within the agency, due to cultural stigma. Instead, they often spoke of seeking counseling from their pastors (most often not trained counselors). I started to think that if there was a way to combine pastoral skills with counseling skills, the clients could be better served. I looked at several programs in counseling, but most of them felt focused on the mind alone as the source of change. I wanted to learn how to help clients more holistically, that is, accessing their hearts/spirit/souls/guts/intuitions as well (whether we use those words in session or not). In 2009, I found Loyola University Chicago's Institute of Pastoral Studies, which offered a master's in pastoral counseling program. It was there that I met a community of professors and students with whom I resonated. Because I wasn't sure at first if it would be a good fit, and because my children were still very young, I started out slowly, taking one class at a time, and as I had more good experiences in my classes, I matriculated as a part-time student. Including internship, it took me three and a half years to complete the degree.

What is your current job and professional title? How long have you been doing this type of work?

I'm a psychotherapist. I have a private practice that I have been building since 2014. After many discussions and much thought in my training, I decided that I did not want to explicitly identify as a *pastoral* counselor. My sense is that many people have had painful experiences with organized religion and are suspicious or skeptical enough of the word *pastoral* to avoid seeking counseling if I had this kind of wording, for example, on my website. However, I feel strongly that my training provided me with pastoral skills on which I draw heavily throughout my interactions with clients. It also gave me a grounding in theology, which has been very helpful as I walk with clients of different faiths and denominations. When I sit with a client who, for example, comes from a more conservative Christian family, and is coming out as LGBTQIAA, I am able to understand the family's frame of reference as well as how the client interprets that theology differently. This helps me be more sensitive in the work of helping the client navigate the delicate ground between them and the people they love than if I had no background in theology.

Spirituality is an important part of my personal life and is what calls me to this work. It drives my quest to improve my understanding and skills, and sustains me through the challenges of this work. Whether or not spirituality is ever named in a session with a client, it is part of who I am and what I bring. I follow each client's lead in terms of whether or not or how their spiritual life is named or brought into the room. On the occasions when I do outreach to leaders of local faith communities, I do speak with them about my background in pastoral counseling so that they will understand that I am trained to be sensitive to spiritual issues and faith identities their congregants may wish to explore in counseling.

Please describe the environment(s) you work in. What are some of the pros and cons of the environment(s)?

I share office space with several other therapists in private practice. The advantages of this situation is that I am in charge of my own practice: I get to set my own schedule, decide which clients to take and which to refer out, how to set my fees, which insurance companies I want to deal with, how to manage my sliding scale, and how I want to do outreach. I appreciate the lack of office politics, the flexibility I have to make changes as I see fit, and the ability to seek my own supervision/consultation from the people I choose.

The disadvantages include the administrative work, which I have largely done myself. Although I paid someone to help with billing and setting up systems for a time, I have had to learn a lot of administrative things the hard way and have had some expensive and difficult lessons along the way. Navigating the credentialing process with insurance companies was particularly frustrating, and I envied colleagues who had administrative people to do their paneling and billing work for them. Also, being in private practice can be isolating. I do not have much interaction with my office mates as we all work behind closed doors. To remedy this, I sought out a consultation group made up of other therapists in private practice, and that has been a significant source of connection and support.

Please describe a typical day/week at your job.

I often arrive at my office half an hour before my first client and take some time to settle in and review my schedule of clients for the day. I recall some of the issues I have discussed with each and think about possibilities for the session, while remaining aware that the client may walk in with something different in mind that will lead us in another direction. I take a few moments to breathe and center myself before the client arrives, to let go of other tasks and concerns so that I can focus on the person in front of me. I typically have 4–7 clients in a day and schedule between 5 and 55 minutes of break in between clients. If I only have 5 minutes, I make sure to move around during that time. After my last client, I write notes about each session and then return calls and e-mails. On days when I have fewer clients, I catch up with administrative tasks such as checking benefits with insurance providers, submitting or troubleshooting claims and invoices, and dealing with income and expenses.

What are the best and worst parts of your job and profession?

The best parts of my job and profession center around making a difference in people's lives. Clients come to therapy because they are uncomfortable and/or upset about something (or several things) in their lives. I feel blessed to be able to help people develop the inner tools and capacities to address their problems, examine their patterns and histories, rewrite their narratives, and develop a stronger sense of internal anchoring. It is extremely satisfying to work with people over time and hear them reflect on how they have changed the way they act or respond to their lives as a result of their work in therapy and how they are feeling relief, improvement, and progress. I also love that I spend much of my day in deep conversations, exploring people's interior landscapes and standing with them on what feels like sacred ground. I feel honored to be trusted with the stories and feelings people share.

The worst part of the job and profession is the inequitable access to health care in this country. It is frustrating to deal with insurance companies in the current economy and how they profit by offering as little care as possible to their members while charging ever-increasing premiums and deductibles. The insurance providers also make it so difficult to navigate the system that even the savviest clients often don't understand their coverage (or lack thereof). While offering a sliding scale helps me to reach people who are uninsured or underinsured, it is difficult for me to make a living this way, and so I always need to balance my client load. I have learned more about insurance than I ever wanted to, and it is always changing and getting more complicated for me as the provider as well as my clients to navigate successfully. I would like to become a Medicaid provider, but despite many months spent in pursuit of this, it seems as though LCPCs are for some reason not eligible, which is a great disappointment.

What would have been helpful to know when you first embarked upon this career?

It would have been helpful to know more about the landscape of professional settings. In teaching students in the MAPC program who are preparing for internship, I have been struck by how many of them have been told that their pastoral orientation is not welcomed in an agency. I have also known colleagues who identified as pastoral and did not succeed in marketing their private practices. It would have been helpful to know how much stigma against pastoral counseling is in the population and within the counseling community itself and how pastoral counselors can manage this by leaving off language that may be misinterpreted in job applications and marketing materials.

What should individuals exploring this career consider in order to make the best decision?

Individuals exploring this career may want to think about their own faith identities and how this is likely (or not) to impact their practice of counseling. For example, many students in my program were part of religious orders that were sponsoring their education. As such, their career trajectories were fairly clear; they would go back to work for the parish or congregation or diocese with whom they were affiliated. For those who were not "religious" in this sense or were not Christian, the interplay between faith and faith community was less clear. If an individual has a spiritual practice but is not part of a faith community, I would ask them to think about where they will find conversation partners to provide support and community as they go through the training as a potential minority in their programs. It would also be helpful to research a program to learn about the diversity of its students and course offerings.

What is the best preparation for individuals considering this field?

I would suggest that an individual considering the field do a thorough exploration of the different training programs offered and ask each program to provide the contact information of alumni who represent as broad a spectrum as possible in terms of their faith orientation and professional setting.

(A. Toback, personal communication, October 8, 2017)

References

Bureau of Labor Statistics, U.S. Department of Labor. (2017a). Substance abuse, behavioral disorder, and mental health counselors. *Occupational outlook handbook.* Retrieved from https://www.bls.gov/ooh/community-and-social-service/substance-abuse-behavioral-disorder-and-mental-health-counselors.htm

Bureau of Labor Statistics, U.S. Department of Labor. (2017b). Marriage and family therapists. *Occupational outlook handbook.* Retrieved from https://www.bls.gov/ooh/community-and-social-service/marriage-and-family-therapists.htm

Bureau of Labor Statistics, U.S. Department of Labor. (2017c). Occupational projections and worker characteristics: Clergy. Retrieved from https://www.bls.gov/emp/ep_table_107.htm

GoodTherapy.org. (n.d.). Pastoral counseling. GoodTherapy.org. Retrieved from https://www.goodtherapy.org/learn-about-therapy/modes/pastoral-counseling# Limitations

Snodgrass, J. L. (2017). Why pastoral counseling. AAPC.org. Retrieved from http://www.aapc.org/page/WhyPastoral

Walker, K. R., Scheidegger, T. H., End, L., & Amundsen, M. (2012). The misunderstood pastoral counselor: Knowledge and religiosity as factors affecting a client's choice. Paper based on a program presented at the 2012 American Counseling Association Annual Conference and Exposition, San Francisco, CA, March 23–25. *Ideas and Research You Can Use: VISTAS 2012*, Vol. 1.

REHABILITATION COUNSELORS

A DAY IN THE LIFE

"Rehabilitation counseling is a systematic process which assists persons with physical, mental, developmental, cognitive, and emotional disabilities to achieve their personal, career, and independent living goals in the most integrated settings possible through the application of the counseling process. The counseling process involves communication, goal setting, and beneficial growth or change through self-advocacy, psychological, vocational, social, and behavioral interventions." (http://www.arcaweb.org/)

Your work as a rehabilitation counselor revolves around assisting individuals, with a range of disabilities, live their lives as independently as possible. While much of your work may be focused on helping clients become employed in order to gain or maintain their independence, it is certainly not limited to employer/career concerns. You will consult with other health care providers to determine an appropriate treatment plan, and you will ensure that your clients have access to necessary medical and community services to remove barriers to independence and employability. You will identify obstacles to client employment, such as inaccessible worksites, inflexible schedules, or transportation problems. Most importantly, you will work with your clients, individually and in groups, offering them "a holistic counseling process that considers the whole person, including the nature of the client's medical condition, injury, or disability; his or her ability to adapt to the situation; his or her ability to live as independently as possible; and, where appropriate, his or her ability to function in a work setting" (Berens, 2009, p. 447).

As a rehabilitation counselor, you may work with a vast array of clients with physical, mental, or emotional disabilities. You may see clients whose disabilities are the result of birth defects, aging, accidents, military service, learning disabilities, autism spectrum disorders, substance abuse problems, or the stress of daily life. You will help people with disabilities at various stages in their lives achieve access to education, housing, employment, and a range of medical and community services. You may find work in a range of settings, depending on the populations you are interested in serving. The environments that rehabilitation counselors work in include community rehabilitation centers, senior citizen centers, youth guidance organizations, state and federal rehabilitation agencies, nonprofit rehabilitation agencies, human resources functions of any organization, schools, insurance companies, or private practice.

As a rehabilitation counselor, you will typically find yourself involved in work that will require you to

- evaluate clients' aptitudes, abilities, interests, experiences, skills, health, education, and career goals and develop a treatment plan in consultation with other professionals, such as doctors, physical and occupational therapists, and psychologists;

- confer with clients to discuss their options and goals, and provide individual and group counseling to help clients develop their strengths and adjust to their limitations;

- arrange for clients to obtain services, such as wheelchairs, computer programs, medical assistance, career training, or any resources that help clients live and work more independently;

- help employers understand the needs and abilities of people with disabilities, as well as laws and resources that affect people with disabilities;

- maintain close contact with clients during job training and placements to resolve problems and evaluate placement adequacy;

- advocate for the rights of people with disabilities to live in a community and work in the job of their choice; and

- prepare and maintain records and case files, including documentation such as clients' personal and eligibility information, services provided, narratives of client contacts, and relevant correspondence.

SALARY AND JOB OUTLOOK

In 2016, rehabilitation counselors held about 119,300 jobs. The demand for rehabilitation counselors is expected to grow at the rate of 10 percent through 2026, due to the increased numbers of elderly and of veterans disabled during their military service. In May 2016, the average wage was $34,670 for people in this field, with individuals in the top 10 percent earning $62,010 (Bureau of Labor Statistics [BLS], 2017). The industries with the highest levels of employment for rehabilitation counselors are:

- State and local government, excluding education and hospitals $47,490

- Individual and family services $33,390

- Nursing and residential care facilities $30,610

- Vocational rehabilitation services $30,410

It is worth noting that a salary survey was done in 2014 by the American Counseling Association (ACA; n.d.). This survey found that the average salary for rehabilitation counselors was $53,561. Their explanation for the significant difference from BLS data is the "many inter-related factors influence salary, among them geography, length of experience, work setting, education, certification, and job description" (ACA, n.d., p. 8). Specifically, 64 percent of the rehabilitation counselors responding to the ACA survey had eight or more years of experience in the field.

BEST PREPARATION

It is particularly important to have experience working with individuals with disabilities before you enter this field. Whether you volunteer or work part or full time in an environment that serves people with disabilities, exposure to the field is critical to making an informed career choice.

In order to obtain a position, most employers require a master's degree in rehabilitation counseling or a related field. A license to practice as a rehabilitation counselor requires 2,000 to 4,000 hours of supervised clinical experience. In addition, counselors must pass a state-recognized exam and complete annual continuing education credits.

SPECIAL CONSIDERATIONS

Some employers prefer to hire Certified Rehabilitation Counselors (CRC). Of the 581 rehabilitation counselors who responded to the ACA Counselor Compensation Study, 90 percent were certified (ACA, n.d.).

Applicants must meet advanced education, work-experience, and clinical-supervision requirements and pass a test. Once certified, counselors must complete continuing education requirements.

- Certified Rehabilitation Counselor (CRC)—See the Commission on Rehabilitation Certification (https://www.crccertification.com/eligibility-requirements) for more information.

ADDITIONAL RESOURCES

American Counseling Association	https://www.counseling.org/
American Rehabilitation Counseling Association	http://www.arcaweb.org/
Commission on Rehabilitation Certification	https://www.crccertification.com/
Council of State Administrators of Vocational Rehabilitation	https://www.csavr.org/

MEET ANDREW HRVOL, MA, CRC, LPC

What has your career trajectory been? What prompted you to become a rehab counselor?

When I first graduated from my master's program, I took a job working in the field of higher education. I worked in disability services for two Chicago-area colleges, where I was interpreting medical and psychiatric documentation, assessing students with disabilities, providing accommodations in accordance with the Americans with Disabilities Act (ADA), and providing counseling. I also provided advocacy for students and ensured equal access to educational opportunities for both schools.

Most recently, I have transitioned to the role of a vocational rehabilitation counselor with a national nonprofit organization that represents veterans with spinal cord injury and disease. In this role, I am part of a national six-member team who works with veterans from all 50 states and Puerto Rico. I specialize in providing veterans, with both physical and psychiatric disabilities, and their families with holistic and individualized vocational counseling and assistance. The services I offer to clients include resume building, career assessment/exploration, skills translation, labor market assessment/job development, interview preparation, and employer networking. I also travel domestically to meet with employers and attend events/conferences, providing disability education and hiring information, as well as workplace ADA assessments.

Before starting my MA program, I worked for the University of Iowa Hospital and Clinics in an inpatient psychiatric unit. Working with patients struggling to manage severe psychiatric conditions solidified my career trajectory in counseling and allowed me to hone my skills and abilities. I chose to attend the University of Iowa master's program because it afforded me with the opportunity to become dually certified as a vocational rehabilitation counselor and licensed as a professional counselor. While working on finishing my master's in rehabilitation and counselor education, I interned with the Department of Veterans Affairs in Hines, Illinois. I worked in a program that provided veterans with temporary VA employment while they worked on their resumes and applied for jobs. I served not only as their vocational rehabilitation counselor but also as a therapist, helping them process any difficulties or overcome any barriers. Once I graduated, I was hired as a consultant for a private company, where I conducted labor market assessment, interpreted medical and vocational evaluations, and determined return-to-work potential on a contract basis.

What is your current job and professional title? How long have you been doing this kind of work?

I am currently a vocational rehabilitation counselor. I am a Certified Rehabilitation Counselor (CRC) and Licensed Professional Counselor (LPC) in Illinois. I have been working in the field of rehabilitation and mental health counseling for just over five years in various fields, including higher education, vocational consulting, and veterans services.

Please describe the environments you work in and the pros and cons.

I currently work for a national nonprofit headquartered in Washington, DC, however, my office is located at the Edward Hines, Jr. Department of Veterans Affairs in Hines, Illinois. I have been in this role for just over a year and a half and love the work. Currently, I oversee a caseload spanning several states that includes clients with and without disabilities. As I work in a large territory, I do a lot of distance (phone/e-mail) rehabilitation counseling. The position that I am currently in affords me the opportunity for frequent travel to conferences, meetings, and events. We are a closely knit team of VR counselors in six different VA medical centers around the country, which means that I work from a single office. Most of my day is spent in an office environment, answering phone calls, attending meetings, and conducting client services.

Pros of the job:

- Attending national events—NVWG, conferences, meetings, employers
- Manage my own office
- Domestic travel
- The clients we serve
- Independence to develop and grow my office in the Chicago market

Cons:

- No coworkers to see in-person
- No structure, so you really have to stay on top of things and be very organized
- Limited advancement opportunities

Please describe your typical day/week at your job.

That's a good question—I don't know that any of my weeks are "typical." For example, I am writing this from a hotel in Washington, DC, right now, but I spent the first few days of this week in my office.

A typical (non-travel) week can vary, but there are some consistencies:

- Answering e-mails, phone calls, and responding to requests
- Conducting holistic Initial Intake Assessments with new clients, which include a comprehensive assessment of military service, disabilities that may impact an individual's abilities to work, barriers to employment (medical, criminal, etc.), vocational history, and vocational goals and desires. Once we have completed the basic history, we build a plan to get the veteran or spouse to his or her desired level of employment.

- Resume development is a big part of my week, as well. I regularly review several resumes, both civilian and federal, and provide feedback and recommendations to clients. I also assist clients in prepping their resumes for job openings.

- Engaging in job development can take a lot of work; during this process, I am reviewing the client's files to examine his or her transferrable skills, goals, and keeping in mind any relevant disabilities, then exploring our corporate partners' job openings and community openings to assess for jobs that would be a good fit. Finally, I am sending reports to veterans for them to review. If they are interested in applying, then I will assist them with updating their resumes and drafting cover letters.

- Employer outreach and networking—meeting with various employers, both local and national, to discuss the benefits of hiring veterans and individuals with disabilities. During this process, I work with the companies to determine the best application review processes and actions for clients working with the program.

- Event attendance—I attend veterans' events throughout the Chicagoland area, which include meetings of other veterans' service organizations (VSOs), networking events with potential clients and organizational partners, meetings of community partners, or attending job fairs.

During travel times, I am flying to various states and engaging in outreach and recruitment, employer networking, job fairs, or education and presentations. In some cases, I have traveled to national company headquarters and provided an ADA assessment of offices to determine whether or not they would be a good fit for clients with disabilities. I also travel to some of our national office events to engage with our company leadership and network with executives.

What are the best and worst parts of your profession?

Best Parts

- The clients—making a difference in someone's life and returning a piece of their identity

- Opening doors and helping people overcome barriers, allowing them to do things that they never thought were possible

- Working with professionals who are equally passionate about the work

- Excellent job growth in the field

- The openness of career paths—you are certainly not limited to work only in the field of social services. There are many transferrable skills that you learn that would make you a marketable candidate in a variety of settings, including HR, schools, insurance, medical or rehabilitation centers, and federal and state agencies.

Worst Parts

- Low wages—we are in this for the love of helping people, not the salary.

- In order to run a private practice, clinical licensure is necessary.

- It can get monotonous and stressful at times.

What would have been helpful to know when you first embarked on this career?

I did a lot of research before deciding to become a vocational rehabilitation counselor. I would definitely recommend that anyone considering the field do their research—gain an understanding of the field, the job duties of a vocational rehabilitation counselor, and figure out how you want to use your degree.

What should individuals exploring this career consider in order to make the best decision?

Going down this career path does not mean that you have to pigeon-hole yourself into a single position as a vocational rehabilitation counselor. There are plenty of ways to adapt and grow into different roles, careers, and companies.

The diversity of career opportunities—I started graduate school with a singular focus of becoming a mental health counselor in a private practice. However, through my diverse experience in so many different professional settings, including the Department of Corrections, University of Iowa Hospitals and Clinics Benton Neuropsychology Lab, and the Department of Veterans Affairs, I decided not to limit myself. I attended a program that was CACREP and CORE accredited, allowing me to be a mental health practitioner and a vocational rehabilitation counselor.

What is the best preparation for individuals considering this field of counseling?

The best advice that I can give when preparing for a career in rehabilitation counseling is to get as much experience as you can in as many different environments as you can to truly understand what you want to do.

Be ready to work—being a vocational rehabilitation counselor is not an easy career. Working with individuals with disabilities can be stressful! It requires that you put in the work, deal with difficult clients, become a strong advocate, and put in extra hours as needed. But, in the end, it is worth it when you are able to help someone regain a part of their identity.

Get some experience in the field of counseling with individuals with disabilities! I worked in an inpatient hospital setting before graduate school, and it prepared me for the career and taught me a lot about myself and what I want to do in the field of counseling. There are national, state, and local agencies that take employees or volunteers, so get involved!

Final thoughts . . . anything else that would be important to know about rehabilitation counseling?

If you are unsure about rehabilitation counseling as a profession, reach out to professionals in the field. Don't be afraid to ask questions, shadow professionals, and learn!

(A. Hrvol, personal communication, October 14, 2017)

References

American Counseling Association (ACA). (n.d.). *ACA 2014 counselor compensation study.* Available at https://www.crccertification.com/filebin/pdf/careercenter/ACA_SalarySurvey.pdf

Berens, D. E. (2009). Rehabilitation counseling. *The ACA encyclopedia of counseling* (pp. 446–448). Alexandria, VA: American Counseling Association.

Bureau of Labor Statistics, U.S. Department of Labor. (2017). Rehabilitation counselors. *Occupational outlook handbook*. Retrieved from https://www.bls.gov/ooh/community-and-social-service/rehabilitation-counselors.htm

12

SCHOOL COUNSELORS

A DAY IN THE LIFE

"Professional school counselors deliver a comprehensive school counseling program that encourages all students' academic, career, and personal/social development and helps them maximize student achievement. Their work is differentiated by attention to developmental stages of student growth, including the needs, tasks, and student interests related to those stages." (Dahir, 2009, p. 476)

As a school counselor you will do your best to live out this mission. Your days will be spent in an elementary school, middle school, or high school and about 80 percent of your time will be devoted to the direct (in-person interactions with students) or indirect (interactions with parents, other school personnel, community resources) service to your students. Through individual or group work with students, you will help them hone skills that are developmentally appropriate, set realistic academic and career goals and develop a plan to achieve them, and identify and acceptably manage social or behavioral problems. You will work in tandem with their teachers and parents to support your students' efforts around academic and psychosocial development. In addition to working individually and in groups with students, you are also likely to teach classes on an array of topics, including bullying, drug abuse, planning for college, career decision making, and more.

As a mandated reporter, you are responsible for identifying and reporting possible cases of neglect or abuse to the proper authorities. You will also refer students and parents to community resources to receive additional education and support for these concerns or other issues.

You will find yourself involved in a range of activities and in the Executive Summary of the ASCA National Model, the American School Counselor Association (ASCA; 2012, p. 3) has identified the following as approved tasks for school counselors.

- Provide individual student program planning.

- Interpret cognitive, aptitude, and achievement tests.

- Provide individual and small-group counseling services for students.

- Counsel students with attendance issues, dress code violations, or behavioral problems.

- Collaborate with teachers to present school counseling core curriculum lessons.

- Analyze grade point averages in relationship to achievement and interpret student records.

- Provide teachers with suggestions for effective classroom management.

- Ensure student records are maintained as per state and federal regulations.

- Help school administration identify and resolve student issues, needs, and problems.

- Advocate for students at individual education plan meetings, student study teams, and school attendance review boards.

- Analyze disaggregated data.

SALARY AND JOB OUTLOOK

The Bureau of Labor Statistics (BLS; 2017) expects an 11 percent growth in the number of school counselors through 2026. While this increase is slightly above average, it may be tempered by diminishing state and local government budgets.

The average annual primary salary for school counselors, as published in the American Counseling Association's 2014 Counselor Compensation Study, was $53,299. This salary does not take into account extra compensation earned through coaching, supervising student events, taking on extra assignments, and so on (ACA, 2014, p. 8). According to the Bureau of Labor Statistics (2017), the highest 10 percent earned more than $90,030. Most school counselors work full time, which is typically 10 months per year.

BEST PREPARATION

In most states, school counselors must have a master's degree in school counseling or a related field. School counseling training programs require students to have a period of supervised experience, such as an internship. All school counselors must have a state-issued credential (called a certification, license, or endorsement, depending on the state) to practice. A criminal background check is typically conducted as part of the credentialing process.

SPECIAL CONSIDERATIONS

The American School Counselor Association recommends that the counselor/student ratio be 1:250 in order to achieve program effectiveness. It is worth noting that the national average for the 2014–2015 academic year was 1:482 (ASCA, n.d.). The ratio for each state is also available on the ASCA website.

School Counselor Certifications:

- National Certified School Counselor (NCSC)—This certification recognizes counselors who demonstrate specialized knowledge and skills in school counseling. NCSCs show their commitment to the school counseling profession and to providing high-quality services to students, parents, teachers, and the community.

- National Board Certified Teacher (NBCT)—Candidates must possess a bachelor's degree, a valid state teaching license, and three years of classroom or school counselor experience prior to starting the certification process.

ADDITIONAL RESOURCES

American Counseling Association	https://www.counseling.org/
American School Counselors Association	https://www.schoolcounselor.org/
National Board for Certified Counselors	http://www.nbcc.org/
National Board for Professional Teaching Standards	http://www.nbpts.org

MEET MATT SHEAHAN, MED

Please describe your career trajectory.

My first job out of college was working in a psychiatric day treatment program for severely and persistently mentally ill adults. This was a tremendous education. I had little academic work in college that had truly prepared me in any real way for that job. Working with those clients, however, taught me an incredible amount about the heartbreaking intersection of humanity and mental illness. It also awoke in me a deep and abiding respect for LCPCs and social workers, who comprised all of my colleagues. I had no business, neither the education, training, nor professional bearing, to be working among those wonderful people (almost exclusively women), and yet they welcomed me with open arms into their community.

I left social service after nearly two years to work at my alma mater, in the admission office. I spent six years traveling across Illinois and Wisconsin recruiting students. I used my tuition benefits to earn a master's degree in higher education. I became involved in the Illinois Association of College Admission Counselors, an organization that boasts equal membership of high school counselors and college enrollment management professionals. Through these experiences and my desire to connect with students for longer than an admission cycle, I realized that I truly wanted to be a school counselor; so I went directly from my higher ed classes to school counseling classes.

When only my internship and practicum remained to complete my studies, I was fortunate to parlay my admission experience into a full-time position as the college counselor at an independent school on the south side of Chicago. My graduate program agreed to allow this work to count toward my internship and practicum hours. At the end of that first year, I finished my program and earned my certification. While remaining in that role, I searched for opportunities at large public high schools as I felt better suited serving all students instead of just those that could afford private school tuition. I became adept at securing interviews, and made it through multiple rounds on several occasions, but my experience at an independent school of 150 students was an issue that interview panels had difficulty looking beyond.

Over three years into my career, I was offered an opportunity to serve as an "at-risk" counselor at a very poor public high school in the southeastern suburbs. I felt this could be a bridge opportunity. Yes, I could successfully work with rich kids that aspire to go to Stanford, but I could also serve the needs of a 19-year-old teen mom who just wants to graduate before she ages out. The federal grant was for five years, so I knew it was temporary. However, after my first year there, the grant renewal moved to an annual cycle. That level of instability compelled me to search for a job again. I was fortunate to find a generalist position in a large suburban system, where I literally got to do all of the things I wanted to do, including the at-risk and college piece. After a couple of years there, I moved to a very similar position, albeit with a very different population, at my current school. This past year, having finished my grad work 10 years prior, I completed the three additional courses I needed to sit for my LPC and I take the exam soon.

What is your job and professional title? How long have you been doing this type of work?

I am a school counselor. I am in my 11th year of working as a counselor at the secondary level.

Please describe the environment(s) you work in.

Currently, I have a caseload of 325 students in a suburban high school of 4,000. Our school serves the poorest side of a very large town some 30 miles west of Chicago. Our population is approximately 85 percent Latino; 100 percent of our students receive free breakfast and lunch; our graduation rate is below 75 percent.

My previous school was a suburban high school, with 2,800 students. My caseload was 400+ students. Our student population was more affluent. Two-thirds of the student body identified as Caucasian. Our graduation rate was over 95 percent.

In the district prior to that, two-thirds of our student population was African American, with the remaining third primarily Caucasian. The high school met the federal definition of a "Drop-Out Factory," with a graduation rate lower than 60 percent. The poverty there was worlds beyond my current district, as that school served students from some of the poorest communities in the United States.

The first school I worked at was a K–12 private independent school with a 2008 tuition cost of over $20,000. As the college counselor, I dealt with the aspirations of students who were Ivy League bound, or thought they should be. The school itself was surprisingly culturally diverse—over 50 percent of the student body were people of color. What it lacked was true economic diversity. Everyone there graduated and went to a four-year college. The entire upper school population consisted of 150 students.

What are some of the pros and cons of the environment(s)?

Ideally, I would work somewhere that has strong a representative student body across all ranges of cultural identity, socioeconomic status, and academic ability. My current school is not diverse, despite meeting the typical connotation as a primarily Latino-serving institution, as nearly all our students come from impoverished Mexican American families. The private school was diverse culturally, but not at all socioeconomically.

I also value diversity in the performance of the roles of my position. I want to do everything. I want my skillset to be broad and deep. In that regard I strongly prefer my work as a counselor at my last two jobs over my work as a specialist at my first two schools.

One thing I definitely have realized is that all schools, big or small, rich or poor, public or private, are subject to the whims and delusions of those that run them. As such, any shake up at the top threatens everyone underneath. Politics are just as common, vicious, and petty at a tiny, well-appointed college-preparatory high school as they are at a struggling public school beset by poverty and violence.

Please describe a typical day/week at your job.

Work starts before 8 a.m. I respond to e-mails or phone calls. Office time is important as I can be accessible to students, but first period typically only serves students in some sort of academic or personal crisis. Barring student crisis, that first hour is often good for collaborative work with colleagues. Second period is often devoted to meetings and programming and planning sessions. We may also run student groups during this time of day or attend collaborative student support meetings with the social workers and deans with whom we share a caseload.

From third period through sixth, students have a combination of either lunch or study hall depending on their schedules. This is the time they are most able to come see us on their own, or we are most able to send for them. In the fall we meet individually to do a transcript review with every senior. In the spring we meet individually with all of our juniors. Toward the end of first semester/beginning of second, all freshmen and sophomores are also seen individually to pick classes for the following year. Throughout the course of any day we may be required to attend IEP or 504 meetings.

At any given time we may have to respond to a student in crisis. In the more serious instances, we evaluate students for suicidal/homicidal ideation, and if needed we meet with parents or take steps to hospitalize the student. When students are hospitalized, the counselors reach out to their teachers; when they return to school, we coordinate a transition/safety plan and manage appropriate follow-up. We also make regular referrals for outside services. When a student death or a district-wide emergency situation occurs, we serve on crisis teams at the high school or are sent to other schools in the district to present relevant information to the students and/or to staff a trauma and grief triage room.

We present to groups of students on social-emotional learning tasks, are always available for parent meetings, facilitate the college admission process, and are responsible for the submission for all transcripts for the students on our caseload. After school, 3:15 p.m., I supervise the testing center, the library, and am an advisor to a student group. Other counselors coach and advise as well.

What are the best and worst parts of your job and profession?

The job is never boring; there is always much to do, and it is often very different from one day to the next. I am able to partner with inspiring colleagues and educators. Everywhere I've worked I've had a ton of autonomy, which I truly appreciate. The job is too big to be micromanaged from above.

I love working with adolescents. It is such a critical time to set them up well for adulthood. I like being an advocate for them at the precipice, knowing the work we do together has the capacity to lead to concrete future benefits. I like having education as the foundation by which I am able to serve the social and emotional needs of my students. The academic and career planning aspects of the position provide the structure to get kids in front of you and provide entry to greater levels of service.

The worst parts? Working in a school is a double-edged sword. If you are at a school without a lot of stability at the top, which seems like every school, you are constantly shifting your practices and foci to adjust to a new superior's expectations. This is, of course, true for teachers as well. What is different, however, is that teachers' bosses started their careers as teachers themselves. Far too often, counselors are supervised by people who clearly have no understanding of what we actually do. They don't realize or understand the extent of our training or the full spectrum of our work.

What would have been helpful to know when you first embarked upon this career?

I did not fully appreciate how difficult finding a job would be; how limited your opportunities are; how little room you have to be discerning in your search. The perceived quality of the school does not at all reflect the quality of the faculty or counselors under its employ. Let that notion go. Some of the best people I have had the pleasure to work with have spent their career helping deserving kids at "bad" schools. On the other hand, I have never failed to be disappointed by some of the uninspiring dullards that have been coasting since they got tenure at 27 at some of the "great" schools out there.

As there are so few openings out there, I know a lot of graduate programs now offer dual programs where people earn their LPC and their school counseling certification at the same time. I highly recommend pursuing a program like this. Even if you are 100 percent committed to being a school counselor, having the LPC will open doors and provide flexibility.

What should individuals considering this career consider in order to make the best decision?

This career is a calling. You have to be able to do all of it. We are not academic advisors, just helping kids pick classes. We are not college or career coaches, specializing only in what happens after high school. We are not therapists, holding weekly counseling appointments with clients where we explore their inner demons and past traumas. We are, in fact, none of those things and all of those things—and more. If you love social-emotional work, but don't care about the academic piece, or can't keep up with deadlines and paperwork, this is not the job for you. Similarly, if you just want summers off but don't want to have to take grading home with you, or you really just want to coach, don't be a counselor. That's what driver's ed departments are for.

What is the best preparation for individuals considering this field?

I honestly believe you should do something first, before being a counselor. There are some people who could go straight through undergrad to a masters' program in counseling and manage well enough, but I believe experience—professional, life, and otherwise—is essential to being a good school counselor. It is a rare 25-year-old who can walk into a school counseling department and perform well, especially given the lack of standardized quality in internship experiences.

Historically, school counselors had to teach first. That has not been true, at least in my state, for over a decade. Fewer and fewer working school counselors have classroom experience. In some ways that is probably unfortunate, as teachers are some of our best allies. Teaching or subbing is a great way to get used to the confusing and oft convoluted world of secondary education. It is also a great way to develop a working rapport with students and classroom management skills, a quality many counselors, myself included, lack.

Many counselors start in higher education. As high schools and students and their families push post-secondary planning more aggressively, counseling departments are happy to add a former admission representative to their staff. Academic advisors or college career counselors are also well equipped to move over to the high school side. Similarly advisors, TRiO/Upward Bound staff would have a great foundation for school counseling. People with a background in agency or hospital social services programs, particularly those for teens and adolescents, have far superior clinical skills and training than the average school counseling grad. I know a few people that have started as student service department secretaries while they completed their education. I can think of few other professional opportunities that would give as true a sense of the size and scope of our jobs.

Final thoughts . . . anything else that would be important to know about this work?

My biggest routine frustration with my job is the inefficiency of just getting the kids you need to see in front of you. I have yet to find a school with a perfect system. Even the process of writing out passes and plotting out your day is a time-consuming fool's errand. Students are never where they are supposed to be. The students you often most need to see are the ones most frequently absent. Before I retire I will fix the issue. Whether we implant some sort of vibrating chip in each student, like at Panera when your order is ready, or we beam them to us like *Star Trek*, or barring those advances in technology, develop some sort of student-sized pneumatic tube system, I will find the way to get student to my office in a direct and immediate fashion!

(M. Sheahan, personal communication, October 28, 2017)

References

American Counseling Association (ACA). (2014). *Executive summary: Counselor compensation study.* Retrieved from https://www.counseling.org/docs/default-source/default-document-library/aca-exec-summary-compensation-survey.pdf?sfvrsn=2

American School Counselor Association. (n.d.). Careers/roles. Retrieved from https://www.schoolcounselor.org/school-counselors-members/careers-roles

American School Counselor Association. (2012). *Executive summary. The ASCA national model: A framework for school counseling programs* (3rd ed.). Retrieved from https://www.schoolcounselor.org/asca/media/asca/ASCA%20National%20Model%20Templates/ANMExecSumm.pdf

Bureau of Labor Statistics, U.S. Department of Labor. (2017). School and career counselors. *Occupational outlook handbook, 2016–17 edition.* Retrieved from https://www.bls.gov/ooh/community-and-social-service/school-and-career-counselors.htm

Dahir, C. A. (2009). School counseling. *The ACA encyclopedia of counseling* (pp. 476–478). Alexandria, VA: American Counseling Association.

13

STUDENT SERVICES AND COLLEGE ADVISING

A DAY IN THE LIFE

If you become a professional staff member in a college or university setting, you will likely find yourself working in a division or department related to student affairs, academic support services, or enrollment management. While the student counseling or wellness center is often the first-choice destination for a master's-prepared counselor, there are a wealth of roles and functions that you can inhabit in college and university environments. For instance, you might elect to work in academic advising, admissions, athletics, career development, disability services, diversity and multicultural support services, financial aid, leadership development, learning assistance and tutoring, ministry, orientation and student transition services, residence life, student activities, student conduct, or veterans' affairs. You might oversee student organizations, train and supervise students selected to participate in peer programs, or serve as an instructor for credit-bearing courses related to your department/division.

No matter your job title, you will find yourself using the lens of your institutional role to support and advise students, individually and in groups, as they face a multitude of transitions and crises inherent at their stage of human development. This is certainly the type of work that a master's degree in counseling can prepare you to do!

Specifically, in your role as a professional staff member of a college or university, you will

- advise individual students and/or student groups on topics specific to the scope of your role;

- create, support, and evaluate co-curricular programs and services for students;

- teach academic courses specific to your department or division;

- schedule and oversee programming (e.g., athletic events, academic or career programs, workshops or ongoing groups related to health issues, recreational activities);

- communicate with faculty, administrators, professional staff, and other stakeholders;

- coordinate, supervise, and evaluate the activities of students and staff; and

- plan and administer budgets and produce required administrative reports.

In 2014, according to the *Occupational Outlook Handbook*, published by the Bureau of Labor Statistics (BLS), about 75 percent of postsecondary education administrators worked for colleges, universities, and professional schools, while 15 percent were employed by community colleges. The size of a college or university matters, relative not only to the number of professional staff required but also to the types of roles and responsibilities assigned. "Small schools often have smaller staffs who take on many different responsibilities, but larger schools may have different offices for each of these functions. For example, at a small college, the Office of Student Life may oversee student athletics and other activities, whereas a large university may have an Athletics Department" (BLS, 2017).

SALARY AND JOB OUTLOOK

According to the *Occupational Outlook Handbook*, the average growth rate for these occupations between 2016 and 2026 is projected at 10 percent. In May 2016, the median annual wage in colleges, universities, and professional schools, the industry that employed the most postsecondary education administrators, was $93,270. The median annual wage in community colleges, the second largest industry, was $84,090. The lowest 10 percent earned approximately $51,690, and the highest 10 percent earned more than $179,250 (BLS, 2017).

These salary figures are somewhat skewed by the fact that the occupations in this area range from admissions advisor to provost. In general, entry-level salaries in higher education with a master's degree in counseling and 0–5 years of experience would likely be in the $45,000 to $60,000 range.

Postsecondary education administrators generally have 12-month, full-time contracts; however, some schools may offer 10-month contracts or reduced summer hours. As part of their employee benefits package, many colleges and universities offer discounted tuition for full-time employees and their dependents.

BEST PREPARATION

While a bachelor's degree may be acceptable for some entry-level positions, most student services and advising roles require a master's degree. According to the Council for Accreditation of Counseling & Related Educational Programs (CACREP), "Students opting to specialize in student affairs and college counseling programs acquire a strong professional counseling knowledge base including: history of the profession, philosophy, ethics, theory and assessment, while simultaneously learning about the culture of higher education, its organizational dynamics, and administrative structure" (CACREP, n.d.).

Employers typically prefer candidates who have several years of experience in a college setting. Working in any university office, in a peer program, in a leadership role for a student organization, or as a resident assistant while an undergraduate or graduate student are typical ways to gain important experience and create a network that will be invaluable to your job search.

SPECIAL CONSIDERATIONS

While enrollment is expected to increase in higher education, employment growth in public colleges and universities is affected by the constraints placed on state and local government budgets. When funding is reduced, it is not unusual for these institutions to freeze hiring. In some cases, current employees may find themselves being furloughed or laid off.

ADDITIONAL RESOURCES

American College Counseling Association — http://www.collegecounseling.org/

American College Personnel Association — http://www.myacpa.org/

NASPA, Student Affairs Administrators in Higher Education — https://www.naspa.org

There are also numerous professional associations on the regional and national levels that focus on specific occupations (e.g., admissions, residence life, academic advising).

MEET CATHERINE CARRIGAN, MA, JD

What is your job and professional title? How long have you been doing this type of work?

My title is academic advisor and lecturer at Northwestern University School of Communication, and I have been doing this work for five years.

Please describe your career trajectory.

I began my career as an attorney, but I left that field in search of work that was more collaborative and less combative. I earned my counseling degree in my late 20s, and was grateful for the life experience I was able to bring to that program. Immediately after graduation, I spent five years as a career counselor with undergraduates, graduate students, and alumni of a large urban university. A friend encouraged me to apply for my current position because he knew I enjoyed working with students and thought I would enjoy the faculty role offered at my current university. He was correct!

Please describe the environment you work in. What are some of the pros and cons of the environment?

I work in a building that houses both faculty offices and classrooms. I am lucky to have a private office that allows for confidential meetings, and students often stop by on their way to and from classes. Other members of our advising team are spread out across campus, so I only see my direct colleagues once a week at our staff meetings.

Please describe a typical day/week at your job.

I spend the majority of my week conducting individual meetings with students to discuss academic progress, co-curricular involvement, and internship or other work experiences. I serve on cross-campus committees related to issues I care deeply about, including a group focused on improving the experiences of low-income and first-generation students. An average week is also likely to include a faculty meeting or other interaction with professors to help them troubleshoot issues with students. In addition to these duties, I teach an academic internship course for students pursuing work in the communications field.

What are the best and worst parts of your job and profession?

From the outside, academic advising could seem like a dry, administrative position (sign here, file this form there, etc.), and there are certainly days that the recordkeeping can feel tedious. But the best part of my job is getting to know students over the entire length of their time in college. As someone who places a high value on the role of education, I am glad to witness students' intellectual development as well as their psychosocial and professional development.

Most of all, though, I enjoy this role because I can bring my authentic self to it every day—I am able to share more of my life with my students than I would in a more traditional clinical setting. It could just be how many aspiring comedy writers I advise, but I spend a *lot* of my day laughing, and I'm so grateful for that.

What would have been helpful to know when you first embarked upon this career?

Positions like mine can be hard to come by, and universities vary widely in the backgrounds they seek for their advising teams. In interviews, I found that people often wanted to discuss my time as a lawyer, even though I believed my roles counseling and working in academic affairs were my greatest qualifications. Whatever your experience prior to entering this field may be, you should be prepared to explain how you can translate it to an academic setting.

What should individuals exploring this career consider in order to make the best decision?

Working at a university means that you are following the rhythm of the school year. Certain times are consistently very busy and others are less so. You should strive to understand the institution's students—both the "typical student" and those that might be operating at its margins.

The majority of academic advisors are staff members, not faculty, and the salaries can be surprisingly modest.

What is the best preparation for individuals considering this field?

I would strongly encourage students to pursue internships or practica in a college setting, and to get involved in their own programs' administration in whatever ways possible.

Final thoughts . . . anything else that would be important to know about this work?

I think a counseling degree is good preparation for any job that requires significant work with college students, but it is important to maintain good professional boundaries. I am students' academic advisor, not their therapist, and I don't hesitate to refer students to campus counseling services when I believe it is in their best interest. That said, my clinical training and comfort talking about mental health issues have been a huge asset in my current position.

(C. Carrigan, personal communication, October 4, 2017)

References

Bureau of Labor Statistics, U.S. Department of Labor. (2017). Postsecondary education administrators. *Occupational outlook handbook, 2016–17 edition*. Retrieved from https://www.bls.gov/ooh/management/postsecondary-education- administrators.htm

Council for Accreditation of Counseling & Related Educational Programs (CACREP). (n.d.). *For students: Choosing a graduate program*. Retrieved from http://www.cacrep.org/for-students/

MORE CAREER OPTIONS AND FINAL REFLECTIONS

COUNSELORS AND HUMAN RESOURCES

Two of the chapters in this book are devoted to counselors who are often employed by human resources divisions in organizations. While rehabilitation counseling takes place in many different environments, in human resources, rehabilitation counselors "meet with employers and attend events/conferences, providing disability education and hiring information, as well as workplace ADA assessments," as Andrew Hrvol points out in Chapter 11. Organizational counselors work primarily out of human resources and, as Rick Rittmaster tells us in Chapter 9, "it's often a balance between meeting individual needs and supporting [organizational] goals and objectives." There are other roles in human resources that counselors can occupy. Two more are briefly outlined here.

Employee Assistance Counselors

According to the International Employee Assistance Professionals Association (EAPA; 2011), an employee assistance program (EAP) "is a workplace program designed to assist: (1) work organizations in addressing productivity issues, and (2) 'employee clients' in identifying and resolving personal concerns, including health, marital, family, financial, alcohol, drug, legal, emotional, stress, or other personal issues that may affect job performance." Employees contact their EAP programs voluntarily to take advantage of confidential services including assessments, short-term counseling, referrals, and follow-up assistance. As an EAP counselor, you would also provide crisis and trauma intervention and actively help organizations prevent and cope with workplace violence, trauma, and other emergency response situations (U.S. Office of Personnel Management, n.d.).

EAP counselors generally have at least a master's degree in a mental health–related field; many are certified drug and alcohol counselors. Those with experience in the field may choose to become a Certified Employee Assistance Professional (CEAP).

Diversity Initiatives

In a *Fortune* magazine article on workplace diversity, "Great Place to Work," a research and consulting firm has gathered evidence "showing that when employees look up and look to the left and right what they see they internalize. If they can see themselves, it gives them hope that they will be seriously listened to when approaching leaders with new product ideas, growth opportunities, or simply to connect. This hope fuels increased commitment" (Bush & Peters, 2016). In the February issue of the Society for Human Resource Management's *HR Magazine*, a similar article on workplace diversity quotes a 2015 McKinsey & Co. study: "diversity is not just about mirroring the country's demographics. It's also about innovation and performance. Companies that exhibit gender and ethnic diversity are, respectively, 15 percent and 35 percent more likely to outperform those that don't" (Parsi, 2017).

Counselors who would like to be at the forefront of workplace diversity will find varied responsibilities and job titles. In general, you would provide training on cultural sensitivity and recognizing unconscious bias, advocate for diversity awareness through the creation of resource groups and events, and design and implement methods to improve the recruitment of a diverse workforce.

Two associations under the umbrella of ACA that support counselors involved in workplace diversity are the Association for Multicultural Counseling and Development (AMCD) and the Association for Lesbian, Gay, Bisexual, and Transgender Issues in Counseling (ALGBTIC).

COUNSELORS AND ELDER CARE

Gerontological counseling combines knowledge of the science of aging with counseling psychology. As a gerontological counselor you would work with individuals and small groups around issues of elder abuse, discrimination, grief and loss, loneliness, impact of medical problems and physical limitations, substance abuse, financial concerns, and accessing community services for seniors. You could find yourself working in hospitals, churches, nursing homes, senior centers, ombudsman programs, colleges, and government agencies.

The Association for Adult Development and Aging (AADA) is an important resource for sharing, professional development, and advocacy related to adult development and aging issues. It is particularly focused on improving the awareness and ability of counselors to address counseling concerns across the life span.

COUNSELOR EDUCATORS

A counselor educator is typically a licensed professional counselor with a doctoral degree from an accredited PhD counselor education program and professionally versed in counseling, supervision, teaching, research and scholarship, leadership, and advocacy. As a counselor educator you would teach courses in counseling graduate programs; provide master's and doctoral students with clinical supervision; evaluate students in terms of professional competence, preventing those with inadequate skills or inappropriate behaviors from entering the profession; and conduct research.

The Association for Counselor Education and Supervision (ACES) is the premier organization for counselor educators. The primary purpose of the association is to advance counselor education and supervision in order to improve the provision of counseling services in all settings. To that end, ACES focuses its resources on current issues, relevant research, proven practices, ethical standards, and conversations in counselor training and supervision including competencies for supervision and counselor training, research, multicultural competence, and advocacy.

A QUICK LOOK AT RELATED FIELDS

Psychologists

Psychologists are trained to make diagnoses and provide individual and group therapy and may work with severe mental illness. They are not medical doctors, but they do have a doctoral degree in an area of psychology. A psychologist can have a PhD or a PsyD in clinical or counseling psychology. Psychologists may have the same responsibilities as professional counselors, but it is within their scope of practice to offer additional psychological services (e.g., diagnostic testing). While psychologists are not MDs, some states allow psychologists to prescribe a limited number of psychiatric medications if they've taken a course in psychopharmacology (Rehagen, 2015).

Social Workers

Much like counselors, social workers are trained to diagnose and treat mental, behavioral, and emotional disorders and offer a range of therapeutic services to individuals, couples, and groups. Their education also prepares them to work with community groups and organizations and policymakers to develop or improve programs, services, policies, and social conditions. They work in a range of specialty areas and settings. Most social workers are master's prepared (MSW), although there a number of bachelor of social work (BSW) degree programs available as well as graduate programs that also offer a PhD in social work (Bureau of Labor Statistics [BLS], 2017a).

Since this profession is closest to counseling, at least at the master's level, it is useful to make a few comparisons. While a master's degree in social work requires 60 credit hours (similar to a master's in counseling), there are two internships required for a MSW, totaling 1,200 hours. The focus of the coursework is also different, with required social work classes on policy and social institutions that are not typically found in a counseling curriculum. It is also useful to note that social work does not have required courses focusing on career theory or development.

Psychiatrists and Primary Care Physicians

Psychiatrists are defined by the Bureau of Labor Statistics as physicians who diagnose, treat, and help prevent disorders of the mind. They treat mental illnesses through a combination of personal counseling, hospitalization, and medication. Specifically, they analyze and evaluate patient data or test findings to diagnose mental disorders; prescribe or provide psychotherapeutic treatments or medications; design individualized care plans, using a variety of treatments; and collaborate with physicians and other medical and mental health professionals. Psychiatrists are medical doctors who have completed medical school and a residency in psychiatry.

While primary care physicians do not maintain a primary focus on the treatment of mental health or substance abuse concerns, a significant number of individuals will choose the counsel of their primary care physician for mental health rather than contacting a counselor, social worker, psychologist, or psychiatrist. In fact, many people are not aware of the educational and experiential differences that distinguish mental health professionals from each other. Additionally, for many individuals a mental health diagnosis and the need for psychotropic medication are sensitive topics; therefore, it seems simpler to talk to their primary care physician. Level of comfort, ease of access, costs, and insurance coverage are among the reasons why this is the case. That said, many counselors (especially those in private practice) find it beneficial to include primary care physicians in their referral network.

COMING FULL CIRCLE

In 2011, under licensure laws enacted in all 50 states, Puerto Rico, and the District of Columbia, there were over 120,000 licensed professional counselors in the United States (American Counseling Association, 2011). In 2016, according to the U.S. Department of Labor's Bureau of Labor Statistics (BLS, 2017b), there were roughly 1,011,500 mental health professionals practicing in the U.S. Here is the 2016 breakdown (BLS, 2017b):

- Clinical, counseling and school psychologists: 147,500

- Mental health and substance abuse social workers: 123,900

- Substance abuse and behavior disorder counselors: 102,400

- Mental health counselors: 157,700

- Psychiatrists: 27,500

- Marriage and family therapists: 41,500

- Educational, vocational and school counselors: 291,700

- Rehabilitation counselors: 119,300

In each of these fields the projected growth is average to above average through 2024. There are some things these statistics don't tell us, however; and further research would be necessary to discover how many of these jobs are full-time vs. part-time position and what the specific services provided are. Additionally, these estimates usually omit graduate students, interns, and postdoctoral fellows who provide mental health services under the supervision of licensed professionals.

Finally, and perhaps most importantly, these estimates do not include thousands of counselors whose training has helped them find their way into other professions that do not have mental health as the primary focus. In fact, this book has chosen to highlight several of these career options as well.

Why do so many people choose this work? We know the numbers don't tell the whole story. Those of us drawn to counseling tend to be motivated by meaning and purpose over more concrete professional rewards. Helping people, making the world better than we found it, placing ourselves at the intersection of our great gladness and the world's deep hunger (as theologian Frederick Buechner [1993] suggested)—that's what brings us joy. We also prefer variety and diversity in the work we do. Most counselors have worked in different environments, with a number of populations, and many have been involved in several specialty areas.

Matt Sheahan, the school counselor from Chapter 12, also shared his perspective on the agony and ecstasy of a counseling career. His summary seems to say it all:

> The work itself can be deflating and thankless, which I think can be true in any 'helping' profession. Try as you might, as well-intended as you are, your efforts may still be ultimately fruitless. Some kids will still fail, or drop out, or hurt themselves or someone else. Some kids will do everything right and still be derailed by their families, or their neighborhood, or their fertility. You will never feel like you have enough time to do the best job. You will never feel like you gave everyone on your caseload the attention they deserved. You will constantly feel like you are juggling several balls and that, as soon as you get into any kind of rhythm, someone else comes along and tosses in another ball, or a bowling pin, or a flaming sword, or a grenade. When things do come together, however, and all the pieces do fall into place, and your empathetic advocacy is met by a student's earnest efforts to achieve, improve, or overcome, there is nothing more satisfying or fulfilling.

The difficulties of helping professions in general and counseling in particular (as described above) will likely ring true for most counselors. Given that, self-care is critical. No doubt, you've heard about burnout and compassion fatigue. If you plan to do this work, it is critical to accept that (1) you will not be immune to these daily setbacks; and (2) you must actively embrace those things that will keep you healthy and therefore make you better at your job and your life. Peer support and ongoing supervision are the keys to avoiding professional isolation and becoming a victim of burnout. Having a personal life that includes attention to wellness activities as well as room for play and pleasure is also critical to your continued health and ability to work smarter.

If change, variety, and the opportunity to continue to learn and grow professionally while serving others sound exactly like what you've been looking for in a career, then you may find the field of counseling open, engaging, and challenging. It is my hope that this book has served to help you decide whether the profession of counseling is the right place for you. If the answer is yes, then welcome! We are happy to have you join the thousands of practitioners who have found a professional home in the field.

References

American Counseling Association (ACA). (2011). *Who are licensed professional counselors.* Retrieved from https://www.counseling.org/PublicPolicy/WhoAreLPCs.pdf

Buechner, F. (1993). *Wishful thinking.* San Francisco, CA: HarperSanFrancisco.

Bureau of Labor Statistics, U.S. Department of Labor. (2017a). Social workers. *Occupational outlook handbook.* Retrieved from https://www.bls.gov/ooh/community-and-social-service/social-workers.htm

Bureau of Labor Statistics, U.S. Department of Labor. (2017b). *Occupational projections and worker characteristics.* Retrieved from https://www.bls.gov/emp/ep_table_107.htm

Bush, M., & Peters, K. (2016, December 5). How the best companies do diversity right. *Fortune.* Retrieved from http://fortune.com/2016/12/05/diversity-inclusion-workplaces/

International Employee Assistance Professionals Association (EAPA). (2011, October). *Definitions of an employee assistance program (EAP) and EAP core technology.* Retrieved from http://www.eapassn.org/About/About-Employee-Assistance/EAP-Definitions-and-Core-Technology

Parsi, N. (2017, January 16). Workplace diversity and inclusion gets innovative. *HR Magazine.* Retrieved from https://www.shrm.org/hr-today/news/hr-magazine/0217/pages/disrupting-diversity-in-the-workplace.aspx

Rehagen, T. (2015). *Psychologist or psychiatrist: Which is right for you?* WebMD, LLC. Retrieved from https://www.webmd.com/mental-health/features/psychologist-or-psychiatrist-which-for-you#2

U.S. Office of Personnel Management. (n.d.). *Frequently asked questions: What is an employee assistance program (EAP)?* Retrieved from https://www.opm.gov/faqs/QA.aspx?fid=4313c618-a96e-4c8e-b078-1f76912a10d9&pid=2c2b1e5b-6ff1-4940-b478-34039a1e1174